TREASURES FROM THE NATIONAL LIBRARY OF IRELAND

The main Reading Room

TREASURES

FROM THE
NATIONAL LIBRARY
OF IRELAND

Edited by Noel Kissane

PRESENTED BY
THE BOYNE VALLEY HONEY COMPANY
1994

First published in 1994 by The Boyne Valley Honey Company
Reprinted 1995

© The Boyne Valley Honey Company under licence from the
National Library of Ireland

A catalogue record for this book is available from the British Library

ISBN 0 951782 34 7 (paper)
ISBN 0 951782 35 5 (cloth)

Designed by Jarlath Hayes
Photography by Eugene Hogan, National Library
Typeset by Reepro
Printed by Betaprint Ltd

CONTENTS

ACKNOWLEDGEMENTS

The National Library and the publisher are most grateful to the following who contributed to the book by providing specialist information on particular aspects: John Andrews, Clara Bartley, Charles Benson, Gerry Browner, Patricia Butler, Edward Chandler, Seán Connolly, Stephen Coonan, Maurice Craig, Pádraig de Brún, Paul Doyle, Mairead Dunlevy, Patrick Farrell, Luke Gibbons, John Goldsmith, Peter Harbison, Anthony Hughes, Timothy Jackson, Helen Kavanagh, Mary Kelleher, Neil Kennedy, Vincent Kinane, Seán Kirwan, Adrian Le Harivel, Dolores McCarthy, Joseph McDonnell, Alf MacLóchlainn, Seán Mac Mathúna, Edward McParland, Maighread McParland, Catherine Marshall, Bernard Meehan, Nigel Monaghan, Dymphna Moore, Ríonach Ní Ógáin, Eva Ó Cathaoir, Maurice O'Connell, Jim O'Connor, John O'Loughlin Kennedy, Seán Ó Lúing, Stuart Ó Seanóir, Pádraig Ó Snodaigh, Nigel Palmer, Ray Refaussé, Maura Scannell, Hugh Shields, Albert Siggins, Roger Stalley, John Turpin, Patrick Wyse Jackson; to the distinguished historians, Thomas P. O'Neill and Kevin Whelan, both former members of staff of the National Library, who read most of the text and made many helpful suggestions; to the following who were involved in the production of the book or exhibition: Jarlath Hayes who designed the book; Louis McConkey of Reepro for typesetting; Ray Lynn of Betaprint for printing; Fiona Martin who designed the exhibition; Bill Bolger, Maurice Farrell and Paul Callanan of the National College of Art and Design; Muriel McCarthy, Sara McCartan, John Gillis and Matthew Cains of Marsh's Library and the Delmas Bindery; Bord na Gaeilge, especially Éamonn Ó hArgáin; Helen O'Neill and Mary O'Boyle of the Office of Public Works; Tom Durney for frames; Stevan Hartung for display panels; Conor Molloy of Kodak (Ireland) Ltd, and Charles Pritchard and Derek Cronin of the Dublin Microsystems Centre for the Photo CD; Mike Murphy for the audio tape; to three members of National Library staff: Eugene Hogan, Photographer, who provided the photography for the book and exhibition; John Farrell, Preservation Officer, who mounted the exhibition and also contributed to the content of the book; Brian McKenna, Keeper, for the index and other contributions.

Finally, in addition to those who contributed chapters to the book, everybody on the staff of the National Library contributed directly or indirectly and are gratefully acknowledged: Bernard Barry, Teresa Biggins, Noel Brady, John Brazil, Rose Breslin, Christopher Briody, Kevin Browne, William Buckley, Colm Carroll, Francis Carroll, Adrienne Darcy, Thomas Desmond, Bernard Devaney, Margaret Doolan, Michael Drew, Glenn Dunne, James Dunne, Mary Dunne, Alan Dyer, James Fleming, Mark Hardy, James Harte, Marianne Henry, Paul Jones, Anita Joyce, Gerard Kavanagh, Peter Kenny, Sinéad Looby, Sister Frances Lowe, Sylvia Lynam, John Lyons, Philip McCann, Sandra McDermott, Fergus Mac Giolla Easpaig, David McLoughlin, Niall McNamara, Denis McQuaid, Declan Maxwell, Irene Meehan, Carmel Moran, Michael Moran, Marie Moylan, Liam Murphy, Sophia O'Brien, Colette O'Flaherty, Marie O'Gallagher, John O'Leary, James O'Shea, John O'Sullivan, Margaret Reilly, Noel Stapleton, Patrick Sweeeney, Patrick Thompson, Margaret Trimble.

FOREWORD

A treasure, like beauty, is in the eye of the beholder. To select just one hundred treasures from the incomparable resources of this great library has caused much heart-searching and cries of 'but, what about . . ?' The final selection gathered here is the personal selection of the Keeper or Assistant Keeper for each of the chosen categories. Each item has been carefully selected as the most significant or representative or interesting of its genre.

Thanks are due to the individual curators who made their selection and a special commendation goes to Noel Kissane who, like a conductor, brought harmony to the different voices.

This diva pulled rank and sought to have her voice heard. As Director, I can rarely indulge myself by browsing or revelling in the apparently endless delights the National Library holds. This was too good an opportunity to miss and so I have been granted this overture in six parts: my six treasures.

1. My first choice made with total bias and no apologies is a children's book. It was Oscar Wilde who said: 'It's what you read when you don't have to that determines what you will be when you can't help it', and children's books are so difficult to write, so often ignored by the sophisticated adult community, and so wonderful when well produced, that they deserve a section all to themselves. There are so many to choose from – fairytales with jewel-like illustrations, animal fantasies, comic-strip characters now forgotten. With firm resolve I have chosen just one, an early twentieth-century alphabet book for learning Irish. Alphabet books are microcosms of the greater world and we can often learn about the society and the people who wrote them from the things they chose to illustrate them. This example published in 1912, *Coiscéim ar Aghaidh: First Gaelic Book,* by Antoine Ó Dochartaigh, pitches on two animals which were commonplace in both urban and rural Ireland at the time.

aral   bó

a e ı o u á é í ó ú

2. While I am on the topic of alternative treasures, what about all those things that our mothers dubbed 'rubbish' and swept quickly into bins? It is truly a case of one man's dust being another's treasure. The Library has an interesting and varied collection of such items, by way of ephemera, election posters, theatre programmes and an excellent selection of cigarette cards from the early part of this century. Many of the latter are miniature works of art and cover such subjects as natural history, heraldry, transport, broadcasting and Irish legends.

3. I recently came across this acerbic comment in a learned article, 'De-accessioning and Research Libraries': 'It doesn't bother me in the least that in the future many of my books will stand unopened for many years on end. Counting the number of times a book is used as a criterion of value is to reduce a research library and its purposes to absurdity; on that basis

the most valuable books in it are the telephone books'. (Wilmarth Lewis, *Collector's Progress*, New York, 1951). It just so happens that my third treasure is a phone book. *The National Telephone Company's Directory: Irish Section, 1904-5* is, we believe, the earliest Irish telephone directory, and what a story it tells – of those wealthy or innovative enough to subscribe to the 'apparatus', and where they lived. It may not win a design of the year award, but we would be very much the poorer without it. My only problem is that I can locate the National Children's Hospital, the National Electrical Wiring Company, the National Maternity Hospital, but not the National Library.

4. The *Livre d'Artiste* is a species of 'book beautiful' rarely found in Ireland for the very obvious reasons of cost and a small market and, indeed, the lack of interest in the book arts. As an endangered species, rare examples deserve to be seen and shared. *Squarings: Twelve Poems by Seamus Heaney, Four Lithographs by Felim Egan* (Hieroglyph Edition, 1991) should be celebrated with fanfares, uniting, as it does, a great poet, a fine artist, hand-made paper, fine typography and binding – together creating a work of art which can be held and cherished in a very private way.

5. They say that every fisherman and woman remember their first catch. I remember vividly the first major purchase that I influenced, for two reasons. Firstly, it is a rare and beautiful example of one of Ireland's finest illustrators: Dicky Doyle who is best known for his illustrations for *Punch* in the 1840s and for his winsome and charming drawings, *In Fairyland*. My choice is from a small, beautifully-bound volume of unpublished water-colours by the Doyle family; the drawing is untitled – but I have affectionately

dubbed it 'Ant in a Bonnet'. The second reason I remember this purchase is because the monies to purchase it were generously given by a donor who chose to remain anonymous.

6. My final treasure is possibly the rarest of all, a dying and threatened species. I refer to The Donor – often depicted kneeling to the right or left of the Virgin or Saint in medieval books of hours, but in these last years of this century too often unsung. Our sponsor is a perfect example, bringing as he does not just the funds to make this book and exhibition of the Treasures of the National Library a reality, but his enthusiastic, constructive comments and fresh vision. This has been a true partnership between Malachy McCloskey, Boyne Valley Honey Company and the National Library through which we can share with you the treasures we hold in trust. The only fit way to mark our appreciation for this support is to end, as many a medieval scribe did, by writing it in the book:

A Prayer For Malachy McCloskey
and Boyne Valley Honey Company
who Sponsored this Book,
and Pat Donlon
who Wrote this Foreword
AMEN

April 1994

INTRODUCTION

These treasures from the National Library of Ireland are drawn from over one thousand years of history, and represent many strands of human endeavour and cultural achievement. They come from the four corners of Ireland, from Britain and continental Europe, the United States and Australia. They have made their way, often by circuitous and hazardous routes, and have now converged and found sanctuary in Kildare Street. Some arrived in pristine condition, others in various stages of disintegration. Since arriving, they have received basic first-aid and restoration by way of cleaning, possibly fumigation or deacidification, and in many cases physical patching and repair. Some have been bound or rebound between hard covers and now stand shoulder to shoulder with their fellows on the twelve miles of shelving; others are mounted on card and also stand to attention, upright, in solander boxes; the large-sheet items lie flat in drawers or hang suspended in metal cabinets. Each one is perpetually on call, awaiting the summons to the reader in one or other of the reading rooms who hopes, perhaps in vain, that it will provide the required information.

To provide a representative sample of the treasures of the National Library, a certain number has been selected from each of the main collections. While facilitating the selection process, this classified approach enables the items to be presented in context, and to some extent the book may serve as a general guide to the holdings of the National Library. In the case of many of the treasures, the extract which is reproduced is merely representative and is intended to focus attention on a volume, a collection, or the entire file of a particular newspaper.

THE (ROYAL) DUBLIN SOCIETY LIBRARY

Of the one hundred treasures, over sixty predate the foundation of the National Library in 1877. A large number also predate its parent body, the Royal Dublin Society (named the Dublin Society from 1731 to 1820) from which it derived the nucleus of its collections. Of these older treasures, many remained in private ownership for centuries until they were eventually acquired by the RDS Library or the National Library through purchase or donation.

The Dublin Society was established in 1731 by an enlightened group concerned with promoting the Irish economy; its well-publicised aim was 'the improvement of husbandry, manufactures and other useful arts and sciences'. In its very first year, it made provision for a library for the use of members. The acquisitions policy of the Dublin Society Library reflected the aims of the Society, and the main emphasis was on agriculture, science and technology. Many of the members, however, had broader interests and from

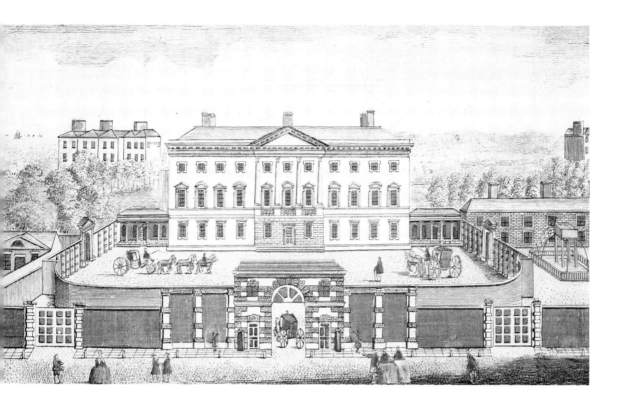

Leinster House; designed by Richard Castle (Cassels) for the Earl of Kildare, it was built *c.*1745 and was originally named Kildare House. (John Rocque, *Survey of the City, Harbour, Bay and Environs of Dublin*, 1757.)

the beginning subject areas such as history, topography and travel were also represented.

The Society changed premises a number of times, and in 1814 it purchased Leinster House in Kildare Street from the Duke of Leinster. This provided relatively spacious accommodation for the Library which then consisted of a little over 10,000 volumes. At the time, the Society received a state grant of £10,000 a year, and as a result its affairs were subject to public scrutiny. In particular, in 1836 a Select Committee of the House of Commons under the chairmanship of William Smith O'Brien focused attention on the Library. It recommended that in the matter of acquisitions, 'the selection should not be too rigidly confined to works of mere science, but that books containing solid and substantial information upon every branch of knowledge may find a place there with propriety'. Moreover, it concluded that the Library should function as 'a national library, accessible under proper regulation to respectable persons of all classes who may be desirous to avail themselves of it for the purpose of literary research'. Over the years the Library became more open to the general public, and the acquisitions policy became progressively more liberal.

The concept of developing the Royal Dublin Society Library as a national public library gained currency, and the movement received a major impetus in 1863 when Dr Jasper Robert Joly donated his extremely valuable library to the RDS. Dr Joly was of Belgian and French extraction, and was born at Clonbullogue in Co. Offaly (then King's County). He was called to the Bar but never practised, and at one time held the administrative post of vicar-general of the diocese of Tuam. He was a discriminating collector of books, prints, sheet music, maps and manuscripts; at the time he presented his library to the RDS it consisted of 25,000 volumes. His deed of gift stipulated: 'If a public library should be established in Dublin under the authority of parliament . . . analogous to the library of the British Museum in London . . . it shall be lawful for the said Society to transfer the collection to the trustees of such public library or institution'.

Jasper Robert Joly (1819-1892) by Stephen Catterson Smith, RHA.
(Courtesy of the Royal Dublin Society.)

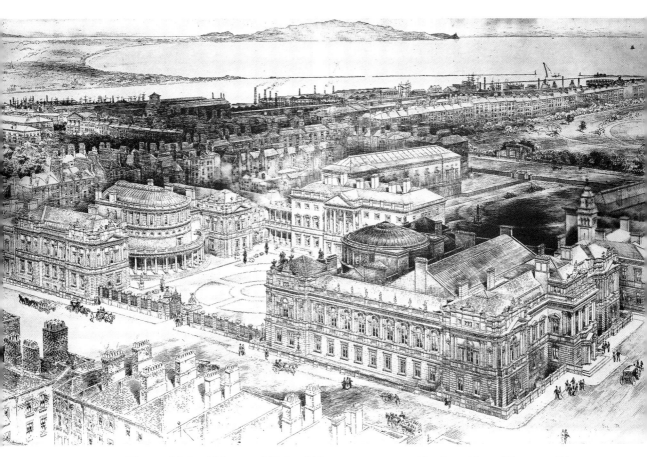

The new National Library and National Museum as represented by the architect. (Courtesy of the National Museum.)

At that point the Government became actively involved in deciding the future of the RDS Library. Under the terms of the Dublin Science and Art Museum Act (1877) and subsequent agreements, it purchased the greater part of the Library and established the National Library of Ireland, with the RDS Library and the Joly Library as the foundation collections. The National Library was to be administered from London by the Department of Science and Art through a librarian and trustees, of whom eight were to be appointed by the RDS. It remained in Leinster House until 1890 when the present building was ready for occupation, although it was not completed for more than thirty years.

THE NATIONAL LIBRARY

The new National Library and the complementary National Museum building were designed in a classical style by the Cork-born architect, Thomas Deane, whose outstanding work was acknowledged by a knighthood on the day the buildings were opened by the Lord Lieutenant. The Library building is itself in many respects a national treasure. It is spacious in design and rich in texture, with fine craftsmanship in masonry, marble, metal, hardwoods and glass. The Library's essential *raison d'être* as a centre of learning is represented by the emblem of the owl and the motto *sapientia* (wisdom) which are set into the mosaic in the entrance hall.

The primary function of the National Library, as enunciated early on by the Librarian, William Archer, and the Council of Trustees (which included Dr Joly), was to act as a national book archive. That is, it aimed to have a copy of every book, newspaper and periodical of Irish origin or interest published through the ages. In addition, it should seek to be encyclopedic and have selections of the literature, the humanities and the arts and sciences of other countries. The government of the day, however, seems to have envisaged a more limited role for the National Library, as a large provincial public library, with only some of the features of contemporary national libraries. In effect, the British Museum was to continue as the national library for the United Kingdom and Ireland; for example, the British Museum was

The entrance hall of the National Library.

5

entitled to free copies of British and Irish publications under the terms of copyright law, but the legislation did not provide reciprocal rights for the National Library of Ireland.

DEVELOPING THE COLLECTIONS

Nevertheless, the collections expanded very rapidly, mainly due to a large number of substantial donations. National libraries tend to attract donations and bequests, and many civic-spirited individuals, societies and institutions presented material; the generosity of the thousands of donors over the years must be acknowledged as an expression of practical patriotism. In the event, the Library proved so successful in attracting material that soon lack of space became a serious problem. Generally, space tends to be a chronic problem for national libraries as, unlike most other types of library, they cannot save space by discarding items as they go out of fashion.

With the establishment of Saorstát Éireann in 1922 and a more sympathetic regime, a number of positive developments took place. In 1924 responsibility for the administration of the Library was assigned to the new Department of Education. In 1926 the building was eventually completed when the east wing adjoining Leinster House was erected. The additional space included an attractive exhibition room which opened with an exhibition of the Library's special treasures. The following year copyright legislation was enacted and the National Library became a legal deposit library for works published in the Irish Free State, but not for British publications which continued to go to Trinity College, as was the case since 1801.

THE GENEALOGICAL OFFICE

A major development in the history of the National Library took place in 1943 when the Office of Arms in Dublin Castle was transferred from British to Irish administration. The Office of Arms dated from 1552, and its archives included records of grants of arms, pedigrees and other genealogical material generated over the centuries. It was reconstituted as the Genealogical Office and administratively linked to the National Library. The distinguished scholar, Dr Edward MacLysaght, was appointed to the new post of Genealogical Officer. The title was later changed to Chief Herald of Ireland.

MANUSCRIPTS AND OTHER MEDIA

In the course of the present century, the nature and scope of historical research has greatly changed. There has been a growing interest in economic, social and cultural history, particularly at local level, and a parallel emphasis on the use of primary documentary sources. In response to the changing requirements

The Department of Manuscripts, the Genealogical Office and the State Heraldic Museum are accommodated in 2-3 Kildare Street.

of its readers, the National Library has developed extensive collections of manuscripts, archival records and other types of documentary material. The Department of Manuscripts was established in 1949, and holds the papers of many Irish writers, politicians and other personalities. Another major component of the manuscripts collection are the records of former landed estates, some of which date from the twelfth century.

The National Library is concerned with preserving information irrespective of the medium in which it is recorded, and has developed substantial holdings of material such as maps, plans, architectural drawings, topographical prints and photographs. For example, in 1943 it purchased the celebrated Lawrence Collection of photographic negatives, and has since had the good fortune to receive a number of substantial donations of photographs. In the late forties, the Director, Dr Richard Hayes, turned his attention to the Irish diaspora and organised the locating, surveying and microfilming of material of Irish interest in libraries and archives in Britain, continental Europe, the United

7

The Manuscripts Reading Room at 2-3 Kildare Street.

States and Australia. As a result of that initiative, many important resources have been made readily accessible to researchers in Ireland.

With diversification into these media, the volume of the collections grew at an unprecedented rate in recent decades and, as a result, shortage of space became an acute problem. The situation has improved with the acquisition of nos. 2-5 Kildare Street which include the former premises of the historic Kildare Street Club. These buildings now provide accommodation for the Department of Manuscripts, the Genealogical Office and the State Heraldic Museum. For the Library as a whole, however, the situation with regard to space and accommodation is still unsatisfactory. Indeed, throughout its history the National Library has been very successful in developing the collections, but it has always lagged behind in providing the space and facilities to house them in fitting conditions.

The collections grow and the treasures accumulate. The achievement of the National Library, however, in amassing these memorials of the achievements of former generations is only a means to an end. As the late Seán O'Faoláin, the distinguished writer and Trustee of the National Library, put it in Kieran Hickey's evocative film, *Portrait of a Library – The National Library of Ireland*

(1977): 'People should think not so much of the books that have gone into the National Library but rather of the books that have come out of it. A library, after all, feeds the people that go in there'.

Many people have indeed gone into the National Library in the past one hundred and seventeen years and, perhaps, its books, manuscripts and atmosphere do indeed resonate in the writings of such regular readers of other days as Beckett, Behan, Griffith, Joyce, Kavanagh, Ó Cadhain, O'Casey, An Piarsach, Synge, Yeats. Their works too, no doubt, will likewise inspire future generations of readers to create yet more treasures for the shelves of the National Library and ultimately for the people of Ireland and the world at large.

EDITORIAL NOTE

1. The bibliographical data for each item generally gives author (if known), title, place of publication (if published), publisher, date of publication or production, size in centimetres, National Library number.

2. Publisher and size are given only where they are likely to be of interest; the Library number is given only where necessary for reference.

3. Measurements are for page or sheet; for those unfamiliar with the metric system, a useful guide is that 30 centimetres equal approximately one foot.

I. PRINTED BOOKS

On its establishment in 1877, the National Library consisted of its two foundation collections (the Royal Dublin Society Library and the Joly Library), both of which were mainly composed of printed books. The RDS Library of 70,000 volumes reflected the Society's interests in having a strong bias towards science and technology. The natural history section was particularly rich and had many eighteenth- and nineteenth-century folio volumes with fine engravings, including Thornton's *Temple of Flora* and thirty-two volumes from Gould's celebrated series on birds of the world. Moreover, the emphasis of the RDS Library had changed over the years, and by 1877 the humanities were relatively well represented. For instance, it included the extremely important set of 300 Thorpe Pamphlets relating to Irish political affairs in the period 1629-1758, which were purchased in 1840 from the London bookseller, Thomas Thorpe.

The RDS Library had a good general collection covering a fair range of subjects, but in terms of the National Library's requirements it was weak in many areas, particularly in works of Irish interest. On the other hand, the Joly Library, consisting of 25,000 volumes, was exceptionally rich in Irish material and included first editions of many seventeenth-century Irish authors. It included a collection of over 700 volumes of sheet music, of which many were printed in Ireland or Scotland. Another of its strengths was the large representation of French works from the Napoleonic period. It also included a number of *incunabula* (literally items from the *cradle* of printing, that is fifteenth-century publications); among the more notable is Schedel's *Nuremberg Chronicle*. An indication of the overall significance of the Joly Library is the relatively large number of items which have been designated as Rare Books within the Library's collection.

While the RDS Library and the Joly Library together amounted to a major collection, it could in no sense be regarded as a comprehensive Irish book archive or as an encyclopedic reference collection of the type appropriate for the National Library. As a result, the Library had to develop its collections from a very low base. The acquisition of current publications proceeded as a matter of routine, subject only to financial constraints. The search for retrospective items of Irish interest published since the dawn of printing in the fifteenth century has, however, proved more difficult and still continues. The main source of these comparatively rare items is the antiquarian book trade which traditionally has had a close relationship with the National Library. Occasionally, a number of retrospective items come on the market at the one time when some long-established private library is put up for sale. A notable occasion was in 1924 when part of the library of the Shirley family of Lough Fea, Co. Monaghan was sold. The National Library purchased some hundreds of items; they included a work on Saint Patrick's Purgatory published at Ulm in 1483; Bonaventura Ó hEodhasa's (O'Hussey's) *An Teagasc Criosdaidhe* (Antwerp, 1611); and the set of 300 Lough Fea Pamphlets from the Cromwellian period which supplement the Thorpe Pamphlets mentioned above.

The acquisition of retrospective titles has been greatly advanced by the generosity of literally thousands of donors over the years. Outstanding in this respect was the distinguished bibliographer, E.R. McClintock Dix, a Dublin solicitor and leading figure in the Gaelic Revival, who presented his collection in the early decades of the century. It consisted of 8,000 books and pamphlets illustrating the history of printing in Ireland. It is remarkable not only for specimens from the presses of the major cities but also for large numbers from the various local presses which operated in the eighteenth century. Of the many private donations of books of general interest, the most notable was the library of Alexander Thom, the printer of *Thom's Directory*, which consisted of 3,900 volumes. In accordance with the terms of bequest, it is maintained as a distinct collection.

As might be expected, many of the volumes have fine bindings. There is also a special collection of over 200 bindings where the covers rather than the contents are the main interest. It consists mainly of bindings from the eighteenth and nineteenth centuries and includes examples from Ireland, England and the Continent. The Irish items attest a distinctive style and constitute an important artistic heritage. In addition to the collection of notable exemplars, the Library is fortunate in having acquired (through the good offices of the National Museum) a collection of rubbings of the splendid series of bindings of the manuscript Journals of the Irish Parliament executed from *c*.1730 to 1801. The Journals and their magnificent bindings were lost when the Public Record Office was destroyed in 1922. The rubbings, executed by the noted lawyer and scholar, Sir Edward Sullivan, have fortunately survived and are a major source for the study of the craft of bookbinding in Dublin in the eighteenth century.

The copyright legislation of 1927 and 1963, which entitles the National Library to free copies of all items published in the Republic, enables it to devote the money saved to other areas. The entitlement, however, does not extend to Northern Ireland. Moreover, the number of books of Irish interest being published abroad is now very considerable as most of our major writers are published in Britain or the United States, and these books account for a significant percentage of expenditure. The acquisition of works covered by copyright also has its problems. While the established commercial publishers generally deposit all their titles, many of the smaller items are published by individuals, clubs, small societies or other groups, some of which are unaware of the obligation to deposit; as the items are usually not widely publicised they can easily slip through the net. Sometimes, however, these items surface again as retrospectives and are then picked up. This was well illustrated in 1967 when the collection donated by the trade union leader, William O'Brien, was found to contain a large number of pamphlets published by various fringe organisations which had not been deposited in accordance with copyright law.

By one means and another, the collection of printed books has developed and approaches a million titles. As there is now a comprehensive public library system and a range of academic and special libraries, the National Library's role is mainly that of an Irish studies library and bibliographical centre. This change in role and function is reflected in acquisitions policy, and almost all the treasures acquired nowadays are essentially Irish.

A Lough Fea Library book-plate featuring the crest and heraldic badges of the Shirley family.

14

1 A fragment of ***Seelen-Würzgarten*** (the herb garden of the soul), Ulm, Conrad Dinckmut, 1483. (25 x 18 cm.)

This four-page fragment from the Library's collection of *incunabula* was one of the Lough Fea items purchased in 1924. It is bound as a volume and consists of three pages of text in German and a woodcut which has been coloured by hand; the woodcut is a representation of hell with the damned being punished for their vices.

The fragment relates to Saint Patrick's Purgatory, the cave on Station Island in Lough Derg, Co. Donegal, where St Patrick is supposed to have fasted for forty days and to have witnessed the horrors of purgatory and hell. The legend became extremely popular from the twelfth century onwards and some versions claimed that certain pilgrims were favoured with visions of the infernal regions. The text is headed (in translation), 'How one may enter Saint Patrick's Purgatory'; it outlines the ritual involved in entering the Purgatory.

At the time this account was published, the site attracted pilgrims from all over Europe, but in 1497 pilgrimage was banned by Pope Alexander VI, on the grounds that it had a superstitious rather than a religious character. Six years later, however, the interdict was lifted, and Saint Patrick's Purgatory continues to be one of the most popular places of pilgrimage in Ireland to the present day. It has also stimulated a large body of literary work, from such figures as William Carleton, Denis Devlin, Patrick Kavanagh, and Seamus Heaney.

15

2 Hartmann Schedel, *Liber Chronicarum,* Nuremberg, 1493. (44 x 30 cm.)

This history of the world, generally known as the Nuremberg Chronicle, was compiled by Hartmann Schedel, a medical doctor and bibliophile in the German city of Nuremberg, then a flourishing artistic centre. The book was conceived as a work of art incorporating aspects of the traditional manuscript codex, to be made widely accessible by means of the new technology of printing. The woodcuts were commissioned from a number of artists, including Michael Wolgemut and the young Albrecht Dürer. The work was printed on twenty-four presses at the great printing and publishing house of Anton Koberger and involved over one hundred skilled printer's journeymen. The work was published in Latin and German editions, estimated at 1,500 and 1,000 copies respectively. The illustration shows Adam and Eve in the Garden of Eden before and after the Expulsion. Many of the plates are hand-coloured but the colouring is late.

The work is outstanding in terms of design, illustration, typography and printing. The text, however, is of little interest as Schedel was uncritical in his use of sources. He dismisses Ireland rather cursorily, merely mentioning that it was partly under English rule and that nothing of note had been recorded of it. He does, however, give brief notices of St Patrick and St Brigid, each of whom is depicted in a woodcut. This copy of the Latin edition was acquired by the Joly Library.

St Brigid.

Ｃuncʒ fuggerente diabolo in foʒma fer/
pentis ‚pʒboparētes mandatuʒ dei tråſ/
greſſi fuiſſent: maledixit eis deus: et ait
ferpenti. Maledict⁹ eris inter omnia anīmåtia
ʒ beſtias terre: ſuper pectus tuum gradierisː et
terram comedes cunctis diebus vite tue. Muli/
eri quoqʒ dixit. Multiplicabo erūnas tuas: ʒ cō/
ceptus tuos: in doloʒe paries filios ʒ ſb viri po
teſtate eris: ʒ ipſe dominabitur tibi. Ade vo dixit
Maledicta terra in opere tuo i laboʒibus come
des ex ea: ſpinas ʒ tribulos germinabit tibi: in
ſudoʒe vultus tui veſceris pane tuo: donec reuer
taris in terram de qua ſumptus es. Et cū feciſſʒ
eis deus tunicas pelliceas eiecit cos de paradi/
ſo collocans ante illum cherubin cum flammeo
gladio: vt viam ligni vite cuſtodiat. |

Ham pʒimus homo foʒmatus de limo
terre triginta annoʒū apparens impoſu/
to nomine Eua vxoʒi ſue. Cuʒ de fructu
ligni vetiti oblato ab vxoʒe ſua comediſſet: eie/
cti ſunt de paradiſo voluptatʒ: in terram maledi/
ctionis vt iuxta imprecationeʒ domini dei. Adā
in ſudoʒe vultus ſui operaretur terram: ʒ pane
ſuo veſceretur. Eua quoqʒ in erūnis viueret fili/
os quoqʒ pareret in doloʒe. quam imcompabili/
ſplendoʒe decoʒauit. eå felicitatis ſue imud⁹ bo
ſtis decepit: cū leuitate feminea fructus arboʒis
temerario auſu deguſtauit: ʒ virū ſuū in ſentēti/
am ſuam traxit. Deinde perizomatibus folioʒū
ſuſceptis ex delitiaʒ oʒto in agro ebʒon vna cuʒ
viro pulſa exul venit. Tandem cuʒ partus dolo
res ſepius expta fuiſſet cuʒ laboʒibus in ſenū ʒ
tande in moʒtes ſibi a domino pʒedictå deuenit.

17

3 Bonaventura Ó hEodhasa [O'Hussey], ***An Teagasc Criosdaidhe,*** Antwerp, 1611. (10 x 7 cm.)

This is one of a number of Counter-Reformation religious texts in Irish published on the Continent in the seventeenth century for the use of Catholics in Ireland. They were intended as a riposte to other religious works in Irish which the Reformed Church was circulating here for proselytising purposes. Ó hEodhasa (*c.* 1575-1614) was from the diocese of Clogher and entered the Franciscan college at Louvain in 1607. He became involved in designing a font of Irish type, presumably based on his own rather irregular style of handwriting, which was first used to print his catechism. The printing was done at a printing house in Antwerp, but that same year the Franciscans set up their own press at Louvain. The page of text has the Ten Commandments. The catechism was among the Lough Fea items purchased in 1924.

4 ***The Teares of Ireland,*** *wherein is lively presented as in a map a list of the unheard of cruelties and perfidious treacheries of bloud-thirsty Jesuits and the Popish faction,* London, 1642.

This item is selected from the Library's extensive holdings of seventeenth-century political propaganda. It was occasioned by the rebellion which broke out in Ulster in October 1641, in the course of which many Protestants were murdered. The long-term effects of this tragic episode in Irish history were aggravated by exaggerated accounts of the atrocities. This account is anonymous. The preface is by James Cranford, a Presbyterian minister who licensed publications under Cromwell's government and often contributed a preface to the works he sanctioned. It is illustrated with twelve graphic and emotive woodcuts by the Bohemian engraver, Wenceslaus Hollar, who had settled in London a few years before. The woodcuts were drawn from a stock repertoire, and were not based on first-hand Irish experience. The Library also has a copy of a Dutch edition published the same year. This edition was acquired by the Joly Library.

Hauing rauished Virgens & Wifes they take there Children & dase there braines against the Walls in sight of there weepinge Parents & after destro; yed them likewise,

5 Maria Merian, ***Dissertatio de Generatione et Metamorphosibus Insectorum Surinamensium,*** The Hague, 1726 edition. (50 x 35 cm.)

Maria Sibylla Merian (1647-1717) was a German natural history artist who published a number of books with hand-coloured engravings of European insects and garden flowers. A collection of tropical insects from the Dutch colony of Surinam on the north coast of South America (to which she had access in Holland) attracted her interest. In 1698 she travelled to the region with her daughter Dorothea.

Surinam had extensive tracts of rain forest and was rich in insect life. The women spent two years studying and painting insects and the plants upon which they fed. They eventually produced the celebrated *Metamorphosis Insectorum Surinamensium* (Amsterdam, 1705). The 1726 edition (with a new title) includes additional material; it has 72 plates, of which no. 60 (engraved by Joseph Mulder and hand-coloured after Maria's drawing) is reproduced here. The text is in Latin and French and there is a title-page for each language.

The plate represents the stages of a particular butterfly from caterpillar to pupa (on the leaf to the left) to adult; the adult is shown from above (in blue) and from the side (on the plant). The wasp-like insect in the centre is a hornet which, according to the text, was feared by man and beast. Maria Merian's insects are not always anatomically accurate; the significance of the work, however, is in its general artistry and its superb hand-coloured engravings. The volume was acquired by the RDS Library.

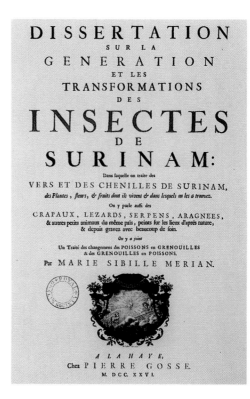

C H A P. VI.

Of the Inhabitants of Lilliput; *their Learning, Laws, and Cuftoms, the Manner of Educating their Children. The Author's way of living in that Country. His Vindication of a great Lady.*

Lthough I intend to leave the Defcription of this Empire to a particular Treatife, yet in the mean time I am content to gratify the curious Reader with fome general Ideas. As the common Size of the Natives is fomewhat under fix Inches high, fo there is an exact Proportion in all other Animals, as well as Plants and Trees: For inftance, the talleft Horfes and Oxen are between four and five Inches

6 The first edition of Swift's **'Gulliver's Travels',** London, 1726. (19 x 12 cm.)

'Gulliver's Travels', as the book soon came to be known, was published on 28 October 1726. It was immediately successful and two further editions were published before the end of the year; as might be expected, the Library has copies of several editions. The pages reproduced here are from a first-edition volume acquired with the Alfred Webb Collection which was donated in 1908.

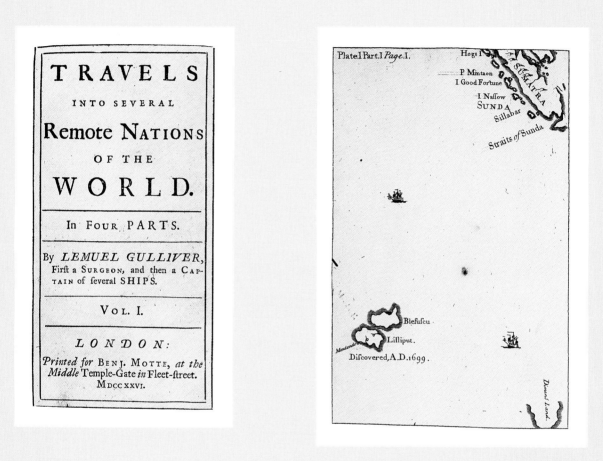

While the book is essentially a sophisticated satire concerned with enlightenment and issues such as the relationship between subjects and rulers and intended 'to vex the world rather than divert it', it has had parallel success as an imaginative work of fiction enjoyed by millions of readers of all ages.

7 Denis Diderot and Jean Le Rond D'Alembert (editors), ***Encyclopédie, ou Dictionnaire Raisonné des Sciences, des Arts et des Metiérs***, 28 volumes, Paris, 1751–72.

This magnificent production is one of the principal literary monuments of the Age of Enlightenment. It was planned, organised and edited by the philosopher Diderot and the mathematician D'Alembert. Its rationale was to outline the principles and applications of every art and science, and it is an outstanding source for the study of eighteenth-century industry, technology, agriculture and arts and crafts. It includes articles by authorities on the various subjects, and is illustrated with plates remarkable for their precision and attention to detail. The complete set was acquired by the RDS Library.

The plate shown here represents in rather stylised fashion a workshop specialising in stringed instruments. Most of the instruments of the period are included and appear at various stages of manufacture.

A contemporary lithograph
by Engelbach.

8 John Field's arrangement of ***The Two Favourite Slave Dances in Black Beard,***
London, [1798].

John Field (1782-1837), pianist and composer, was born at Golden Lane in Dublin
and gave his first public performance at the age of nine on 24 March 1792 at the
Rotunda Assembly Rooms. He later moved to London as an apprentice to the great
Muzio Clementini whom he accompanied to St Petersburg. Thereafter, he lived
mainly in Russia and died in Moscow. Field was one of Ireland's greatest composers
and is commemorated by the John Field Room in the National Concert Hall. He is
best known for his nocturnes which are believed to have influenced Chopin. His six-
page arrangement of the *Slave Dances* was one of his earliest printed works. It was
acquired with a collection of printed and manuscript music donated by Dr H. G.
Farmer in the period 1954-56.

25

Poets still, in graceful numbers,
  May the glowing Roses choose;
But the *Snow-Drop's* simple beauty
  Better suits an humble muse.

Earliest bud that decks the garden,
  Fairest of the fragrant race,
First-born child of vernal Flora,
  Seeking mild, thy lowly place.

9 Robert John Thornton, *A New Illustration of the Sexual System of Carolus von Linnaeus . . . and The Temple of Flora,* London, 1807. (57 x 43 cm.)

This renowned florilegium was conceived, researched, written and published by a London medical doctor, Robert John Thornton (1768?-1837). The most important part of the work is *The Temple of Flora* which has eighteen magnificent colour engravings of flowers. A number of distinguished artists were commissioned to produce paintings of the flowers in their natural settings. The printing process reproduced the basic colours which were then enhanced with watercolour washes. 'Snowdrops' was painted by Abraham Pether, dubbed 'Moonlight Pether' because of his passion for moonlight scenes.

Thornton's descriptions of the flowers are couched in evocative period purple prose and each flower is accompanied by a lengthy poem; the extract reproduced here is by Cordelia Skeeles. The work is of limited scientific value as most of the artists were not botanical specialists, and it is of interest mainly for its fine plates. Thornton published a number of other botanical works, but these ambitious ventures proved to be financially disastrous. Parliament allowed him to organise a public lottery, but even that failed to redeem his fortunes and he died penniless.

10 Edith Oenone Somerville, *The Story of the Discontented Little Elephant,*
London, 1912.

Edith Somerville (1858-1949) is best remembered as a writer of adult fiction in which
she collaborated with her cousin Violet Martin ('Ross'); their works included *The
Real Charlotte* (1894) and *Some Experiences of an Irish R.M.* (1899). She made just this
one excursion into the realms of children's literature. This is a delightful and quirky
work of animal fantasy with a definite moral, and it sits comfortably with books by
such well-known writers of the genre as Rudyard Kipling.

THE DISCONTENTED LITTLE ELEPHANT

Once, very, very long ago,
Before your curls began to grow,
The time when Beasts and Birds could talk,
    (Before you'd even
      learned to walk,)

There lived midst Indian trees and plants,
A family of Elephants.
 The Dadda and the Mummy were
A sensible, old=fashioned pair,
With long grey trunks, and little eyes,
And thick round legs of monster size.
And, though their looks were most absurd,
They uttered no complaining word.

11 The first edition of James Joyce's ***Ulysses,*** Paris, 1922. (24 x 19.5 cm.)

This classic celebration of the adventures of the quintessential Dubliner, Leopold Bloom, on 16 June 1904 was begun in 1914 when Joyce was living in Trieste. While still unfinished, parts of the work were serialised in *The Little Review* in New York and in Harriet Weaver's *Egoist* in London. Eventually, Sylvia Beach, the American proprietor of the Paris bookshop, Shakespeare and Company, published it on 2 February 1922 – Joyce's birthday.

The book was never officially banned in Ireland, but for a number of years it was not generally available here. The National Library copy is number one of the first edition of 1,000 copies. Joyce gave it to Harriet Weaver 'in token of gratitude' on 13 February 1922, and she generously presented it to the National Library on St Patrick's Day 1952.

Stately, plump Buck Mulligan came from the stairhead, bearing a bowl of lather on which a mirror and a razor lay crossed. A yellow dressinggown, ungirdled, was sustained gently behind him by the mild morning air. He held the bowl aloft and intoned :

— *Introibo ad altare Dei.*

Halted, he peered down the dark winding stairs and called up coarsely :

— Come up, Kinch. Come up, you fearful Jesuit.

Solemnly he came forward and mounted the round gunrest. He faced about and blessed gravely thrice the tower, the surrounding country and the awaking mountains. Then, catching sight of Stephen Dedalus, he bent towards him and made rapid crosses in the air, gurgling in his throat and shaking his head. Stephen Dedalus, displeased and sleepy, leaned his arms on the top of the staircase and looked coldly at the shaking gurgling face that blessed him, equine in its length, and at the light untonsured hair, grained and hued like pale oak.

Buck Mulligan peeped an instant under the mirror and then covered the bowl smartly.

— Back to barracks, he said sternly.

He added in a preacher's tone :

— For this, O dearly beloved, is the genuine Christine : body and soul and blood and ouns. Slow music, please. Shut your eyes, gents. One moment. A little trouble about those white corpuscles. Silence, all.

He peered sideways up and gave a long low whistle of call then paused awhile in rapt attention, his even white teeth glistening here and there with gold points. Chrysostomos. Two strong shrill whistles answered through the calm.

— Thanks, old chap, he cried briskly. That will do nicely. Switch off the current, will you ?

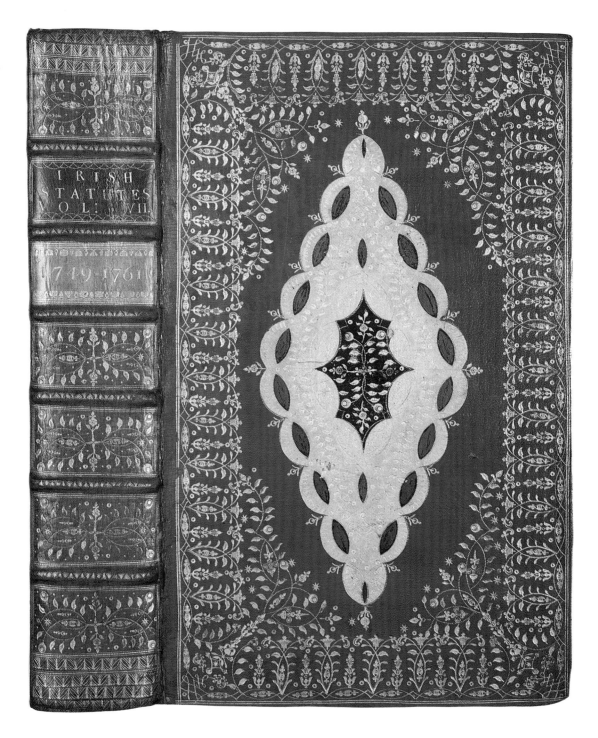

32

12 ***The Statutes of the Kingdom of Ireland,*** Volume VII, Dublin, Boulter Grierson, 1765. (37 x 24 cm.)

This volume is mainly of interest for its handsome binding which is of morocco (goatskin), dyed red. The central lozenge is an overlay of white leather which is stuck on and cut away in the centre to reveal the ground morocco, here stained royal blue. The decoration and gilding of bindings were done with a range of tools, mainly brass stamps, each with a feature such as a bird or flower. The leather was first painted with white of egg (glair) which acted as an adhesive; the tools were then heated and used to press on gold leaf in the required patterns. Borders were generally put on by a roller with a continuous pattern.

The 1765 edition of the statutes consisted of eight volumes. Three sets were lavishly bound for presentation purposes; one set was presented to George III and is now in the British Library. This volume, purchased at Sotheby's in 1935, is from one of the sets which was dispersed at some stage. Another volume from the set is in Trinity College, Cambridge, and five of the volumes were presented to the Irish Georgian Society by Paul Getty in 1986 and are now in Castletown House, Co. Kildare.

Examples of designs from bookbinders' tools in use in Dublin in the eighteenth century. (Maurice Craig, *Irish Bookbindings 1600-1800,* London, 1954.)

II. OFFICIAL PUBLICATIONS

Official publications include diverse material such as acts, statutes, proclamations, parliamentary debates, reports of government departments and a variety of routine statistical data, including census, trade and employment figures. In general, they represent the concerns of government at a particular time, and they also reflect the condition, preoccupations and aspirations of the society being governed. They are extremely significant sources for the study of political, economic and social issues, providing a unique corpus of data for the scholar.

Governments tend to be prolific producers of printed matter and, accordingly, the collection of official publications in the National Library is voluminous. As they are such an important guide to the state of the economy and essential for economic planning, it is not surprising to find that the pragmatic RDS Library built up a substantial collection of Irish and British official publications. These came to the National Library on its foundation and, together with a relatively small number from the Joly Library, form the nucleus of the present collection. In the early decades, the collection was augmented by substantial donations from various institutions and official agencies, as was the case with other types of material. Furthermore, the Library has always actively sought out retrospective official publications of Irish interest missing from its collection and has acquired current items immediately on issue. The collection is now reasonably comprehensive from the seventeenth century onwards.

For the period up to the Union (with Britain) in 1800, the Irish Parliament was the main producer of official publications. Its legislation was obviously of prime importance, and in 1621 a collected edition of the acts from 1310 to 1615 was printed in Dublin. The National Library has a copy of this primary volume and also editions of the complete statutes up to the Union. In addition, it has several volumes of sessional statutes in fine black-letter, that is Gothic type, issued at various times in the seventeenth and early eighteenth centuries. The collection also includes first editions of the *Journal* of the Irish House of Commons (from 1613) and of the House of Lords (from 1634). These provide digests of the proceedings of Parliament on a daily basis. Only a small minority of the issues covered in the debates and legislation of the Irish Parliament were in any sense political. More typically, they relate to mundane matters effecting the economy, such as draining bogs, repairing roads and regulating fisheries.

The Library also has substantial holdings of British official publications from the centuries prior to the Union. For most of that period, the British government claimed jurisdiction here and some Irishmen sat in the British Parliament; as a result, much of the published material, particularly the

the debates and legislation, is obviously of Irish interest and the Library has always tried to develop its holdings.

For the period from the Union to 1922, the official publications of the United Kingdom of Great Britain and Ireland were mainly published in London by the Stationery Office (HMSO). Among the more important for historical purposes are the category known as Parliamentary Papers which are documents laid before Parliament. As they were initially issued in blue wrappers they were generally know as Blue Books. The National Library has a comprehensive collection of Blue Books amounting to 7,000 volumes, which together represent a considerable heritage and constitute a major national treasure. They include various annual reports incorporating masses of accounts and statistical data, much of which is tabulated in a manner which presents regional and local data in a readily accessible form. For the demographic or social historian the census material is obviously of primary importance, especially from 1841 onwards. The census was held every ten years and the reports give population figures for each townland and also data on features such as housing, occupations, religion, language and literacy.

The reports of various parliamentary committees and commissions which investigated particular issues are also extremely informative. Among the more important is that of the Devon Commission (1845) which inquired into land tenure and relations between landlord and tenant. The purposes of the genealogist are particularly well served by Griffith's *General Valuation of Rateable Property in Ireland* (c.1848-64). While this formidable achievement was intended as a statement of the value of each house and farm in the country for taxation purposes, its main interest now is that it provides a complete list of the heads of households by townland or street, and is the starting point in many a search for ancient roots or living relatives.

Time confers a retrospective official sanction on certain documents, the constitutional validity of which would be disputed at the time of publication. This is the case with the 1916 Proclamation and the *Proceedings* of the First Dáil. Not everybody would have regarded them as official at the time, but they are now universally considered as fundamental publications of the State. Since the establishment of Saorstát Éireann in 1922, Oifig an tSoláthair (the Stationery Office) has carried out most official publishing; among its earliest commissions was the first *Bunreacht na h-Éireann* (the Constitution). Today, it publishes the *Acts* of An tOireachtas, the *Debates* of Dáil Éireann and Seanad Éireann and various reports and papers. Irish official publications are also produced by other agencies such as individual government departments and An Gúm, the publications branch of the Department of Education which publishes material in Irish, including school books and children's literature. Nowadays, the National Library acquires all this material under copyright.

The process of government has evolved considerably in recent decades and this is reflected in the area of official publications which more and more are being produced by associations of governments. As Ireland is a member of the European Union and of various other international organisations and agencies, such as the United Nations, GATT and OECD, the National Library receives considerable quantities of their publications as a matter of routine.

Some of the acts and statutes passed by the Irish Parliament in 1695.

THE
CONTENTS

I. **A**N Act for an Additional Duty of Excise, upon Beer, Ale, and other Liquors.

II. An Act for taking away the Writ *De Heretico Comburendo.*

III. An Act declaring all Attainders, and all other Acts made in the late pretended Parliament, to be void.

IV. An Act to Restrain Foreign Education.

V. An Act for the better Securing the Government, by Disarming Papists.

VI. An Act for the better Settleing of Intestates Estates.

VII. An Act for Reviving two Statutes lately Expired, and making them perpetual; and for avoiding unnecessary Sutes and Delays.

VIII. An Act for redress of Inconveniencies for want of, Proof of the Deceases of persons beyond the Seas, or absenting themselves, upon whose Lives Estates do depend.

IX. An Act for the more effectual Suppressing of prophane Cursing and Swearing.

X. An Act to take away Damage clear.

XI. An Act to take away the Benefit of Clergy, from him that doth Stab another not having a Weapon drawn.

❧ By the Queene.

¶ The Queenes Maiesties Proclamation declaring her princely resolution in sending ouer of her Army into the Realme of Ireland.

Lthough our actions and carriage in the whole course of our gouernment, euer since it pleased God to call vs to the succession of this Crowne (being truely considered) may as euidently manifest to all our Subiects, as our conscience doeth clearely witnesse it to our selfe, how earnestly wee haue affected the peace and tranquillitie of the people of our Dominions, and how much we haue preferred clemencie before any other respect, as a vertue both agreeable to our naturall disposition, the sinceritie of the Religion which we professe, and alwayes esteemed by vs the greatest suretie to our Royall State, when our Subiects heartes are assured to vs by the bond of loue, rather then by forced obedience ; Notwithstanding it hath fallen out to our great discontentation, that this our gracious intention in the whole scope of our gouernment, hath not wrought in all mens mindes a like effect, nor brought foorth euery where that fruit of obedience which we expected, and namely in our kingdome and people of Ireland, where (as oftentimes heretofore, so nowe especially of late yeeres) diuers of our Subiects, both of the better sort and of the meaner (abusing our lenitie to their aduantage) haue vnnaturally and without all ground or cause offered by vs, forgotten their allegeance, and (rebelliously taking Armes) haue committed many bloody and violent outrages vpon our loyall Subiects. And though their owne consciences can beare them witnesse that both by vs, and by our ministers there, moe wayes haue bene attempted to reclaime them by clemencie (for auoyding of bloodshed) then is vsuall with Princes that haue so good meanes to reduce them by other meanes, yet haue we not thereof reaped those fruites which so great a grace hath deserued, if there had bene in them any sense of Religion, duetie, or common humanitie. This is therefore the cause that after so long patience wee haue bene compelled to take resolution, to reduce that Kingdome to obedience (which by the Lawes of God and Nature is due vnto vs) by vsing an extraordinary power and force against them; Assuring our selues so much in the iustice of our cause, as we shall finde the same successe (which euer it is the pleasure of God to giue to Princes rights) against vnnaturall rebellions: wherein notwithstanding because we doe conceiue that all our people which are at this present Actors in this Rebellion are not of one kinde, nor carried into it with one minde, but some out of sense they haue of hard measures heretofore offered them by some of our ministers, some for feare of power and might which their aduerse Sects and factions haue growne vnto, by aduantage of this loose time, and some for want of protection and defence against the wicked and barbarous Rebels, and many inueigled with superstitious impressions, wrought in them by the cunning of seditious Priestes and Seminaries (crept into them from forreine parts, suborned by those that are our enemies) and a great part out of a strong opinion put into them by the heades of this Rebellion, that wee intended an vtter extirpation and rooting out of that Nation, and conquest of the Countrey.

Giuen at her Maiesties Mannor of Richmond, the last day of March 1599. in the one and fourtieth yeere of her Highnesse Reigne.

God saue the Queene.

❧ Imprinted at London by the Deputies of Christopher Barker, Printer to
the Queenes most excellent Maiestie.

Anno Dom. 1599.

13 Proclamation by Queen Elizabeth, London, 1599. (41 x 30 cm.)

This proclamation is printed in black-letter type on two sheets. It gives the impression of being written more in sorrow than in anger. The situation facing the Queen was that, in Ulster, the turbulent Hugh O'Neill, Earl of Tyrone, was once again in open revolt. The previous August, at the Battle of the Yellow Ford in Co. Armagh, he had defeated and slain Sir Henry Bagenal, marshal of her army in Ireland. Meanwhile, in Munster, the '*Súgán*' (straw-rope) Earl of Desmond, James FitzThomas FitzGerald, was prosecuting a war against her planters; among the buildings burnt down was Edmund Spenser's castle at Kilcolman, Co. Cork.

The proclamation announces the Queen's intention of sending over yet another army and 'a person to be in that realm the minister both of our justice and mercy'. This was Elizabeth's celebrated favourite, Robert Devereux, Second Earl of Essex, whom she had appointed her Lord Lieutenant in Ireland some weeks before. But Essex proved a disappointment; he failed to gain any significant military advantage and made a truce with O'Neill. As it turned out, it was his successor, Lord Mountjoy, who eventually suppressed the rebellion. His victory at the Battle of Kinsale in December 1601 was the turning point, and a little over a year later O'Neill was forced to surrender. By then, ironically, Essex had lost favour with the Queen and had been beheaded, and she herself was also dead.

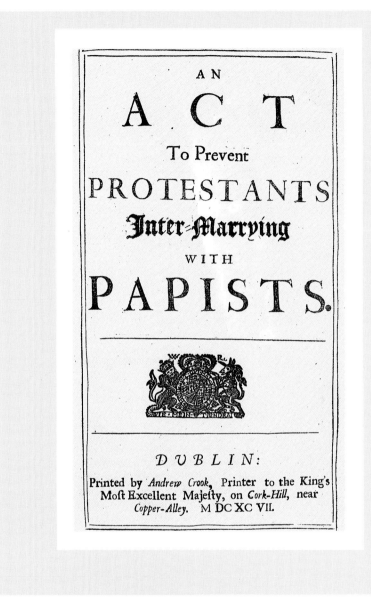

14 ***An Act to Prevent Protestants Inter-marrying with Papists,*** enacted by the Irish Parliament in 1695, published Dublin, 1697.

This is the first Irish statute relating to marriage, but its main significance now is that it is a document which illustrates the political realities of the period. It was enacted in the first decade of the Penal Laws and it was concerned not so much with marriage as with property and its concomitant political power; its aim was to ensure that both remained in Protestant hands. It required that any Protestant woman, owning (or heiress to) property worth more than five hundred pounds and about to marry,

An A C T to Prevent

Proteſtants Inter-Marrying with Papiſts.

CHAP. XXVIII.

WHEREAS many Proteſtant Maidens and Women, as well ſuch as be Heirs Apparent to their Anceſtors, as others, having left unto them by their Father, or other Anceſtor or Friends, Mannors, Lands, Tenements, and Hereditaments, or other great Subſtances in Goods or Chattels, Real or Perſonal, for their Advancement in Marriage; or having had conſiderable Eſtates for Life, by Dower or Jointure, or having had the Tuition or Guardianſhip of Proteſtant Children Intituled to ſuch Eſtates, or Intereſts, as aforeſaid, by Flattery and other Crafty Inſinuations of Popiſh Perſons, have been Seduced and Prevailed upon, to Contract Matrimony with, and take to Husband, Papiſts or Popiſh Perſons; which Marriages have not only Tended to the Ruine and Deſtruction of ſuch Eſtates and Intereſts, and to the great Loſs and Damage of many Proteſtant Perſons, to whom the ſame might Deſcend or Come, but as well to the Corrupting and Perverting ſuch Proteſtants ſo Marrying, and the Proteſtant Perſons in their Tuition and Guardianſhip, as aforeſaid, that

A 2   they

should first obtain an official certificate stating that her intended spouse was Protestant. Women who disregarded the act faced loss of property or disinheritance; clergy or others officiating at an unauthorised marriage were liable to a fine or imprisonment. There are no statistics for the number of mixed marriages in the period of the Penal Laws, but it is unlikely that there were many, and this piece of legislation seems to have had the desired effect.

IRISHMEN,

YOU have not forgot Bantry bay. You know what efforts France has made to assist you.

Her affection for you, her desire of avenging your wrongs and assuring your independence can never be impaired.

After several unsuccessfull attempts, behold at last Frenchmen arrived amongst you.

They come to support your courage, to share your dangers, to join their arms and to mix their blood with yours in the sacred cause of liberty.

They are the forerunners of other Frenchmen, whom you shall soon enfold in your arms.

Brave IRISHMEN, our cause is common. Like you we abhor the avaricious and blood-thirsty policy of an oppressive governement. Like you we hold as indefeasible the right of all nations to liberty. Like you we are persuaded that the peace of the world shall ever be troubled as long as the British ministry is suffered to make with impunity a traffic of the industry, labour and blood of the people.

But exclusive of the same interests which unite us, we have powerfull motives to love and defend you.

Have we not been the pretext of the cruelty exercised against you by the Cabinet of S.t James? The heart-felt interest you have shown for the grand events of our revolution, has it not been imputed to you as a crime? Are not tortures and death continually hanging over such of you as are barely suspected of being our friends?

Let us unite then and march to glory.

We Swear the most inviolable respect for your properties, your laws and all your religions opinions. Be free, be masters in your own country. We look for no other conquest than that of your Liberty, no other success than yours.

The moment of breaking your chains is arrived. Our triumphant troops are now flying to the extremities of the earth to tear up the roots of the wealth and tyranny of our enemies. That frightfull colossus is mouldering away in every part. Can any Irishman base enough to seperate himself in such a happy conjuncture from the grand interest of his country, If such there be, brave friends, let him be chased from the country he betrays and let his property become the reward of those generous men who know how to fight and die.

Irishmen, recollect the late defeats which your ennemies have experienced from the French; recollect the plains of Honscoote, Toulon, Quiberon and Ostende; recollect America free from the moment she wished to be so. The contest between you and your oppressors cannot be long.

Union, Liberty, the Irish Republic. Such is our shout. Let us march. Our hearts are devoted to you; our glory is in your happiness.

15 A proclamation issued by the French force under General Jean Humbert which landed at Kilcummin Bay near Killala, Co. Mayo, on 22 August 1798. (83 x 50 cm.)

The expeditionary force was transported in three frigates and amounted to about 1,000 men; it was small in comparison with the invasion fleet which turned back from Bantry Bay two years before due to bad weather. This expedition was hastily assembled to provide support for the United Irish insurrection. Humbert had been assured by the Directory in Paris that reinforcements would quickly follow.

The proclamation was printed in France and was intended to rally Irish support. This copy has a manuscript note in a contemporary hand on the back: 'Brought by Coln Craffords servant from Ballynemock'. Colonel Robert Crauford was one of General Lake's commanders at Ballinamuck, Co. Longford, where Humbert was defeated. The proclamation was acquired in 1934.

A contemporary engraving.

The Surrender of the French General Humbert
To General Lake at Ballinamuck September 8th 1798.

RIAGHLACHA
AGUS ORDUIGHTHE

OIFIG-AN-CHOGAIDH A MBAILEATHA-CLIATH, An 1d Lá do Nobhumb, An 1806.

Le Arm an Riogh chur an Ordughadh nios fearr, agus leis na Saighdiuraighe bheith a slighe nios fearr, mar ta a Bharrantas an Riogh don 7ª la do October, 1806, agus an Achtaibh airighthe do deineamh an Siosa deireanach don Pharliament.

Am agus Tearma Liostala.

An sna Coisighthe (Infantry) - - - 7 mbliaghna.
Marcsluagh (Cavalry) - - - 10
Ordonas (Artillery) - - - 12
Fir ar mhian leo dul air aigheadh leis an Dara Tearma seirbhise liostalfar airis iad.
An sna Coisighthe - - - 7 mbliaghna.
Marcsluagh - - - 7
Ordonas - - - 5
Fir ar mhian leo dul asteach air an Triughadh Tearma Seirbhise, liostalfar airis iad.
An sna Coisighthe - - - - 7 mbliaghna
Marcsluagh - - - - 7
Ordonas - - - - 5

Ni lualfar do Mhaor na do Shaigdiur liostail air an Dara Tearma Seirbhise, acht air ttaoibh a stigh do Bliaghain do Chrich an Chead Tearma, ionn air an Triughadh Tearma acht a ttogas Dha Bhliaghain do Dheirigh an Dara Tearma, agus ni tuigthear an Tearma Nuadh do thosnuighe a Ceas air bith, acht tar eis Chriochnaithe an Tearma Roimhe.

Ni lualfar do Mhaor na do Shaigdiur liostail airis, na gcalmhuin go liostalfa a Regiment air bith eile acht an a Regiment fein, sol fa leigthear a mach iomlan e.

Ni lualfar do Mhaor na do Shaighdiur, aig dul asaon tSeirbhis amhain, a Seirbhis eile, mar ta as na Coisigithe san Marcsluagh, as in Marcsluagh an Ordonas, acht cheadna, dul asteach Tearma Bliaghan ionan agus an chead Tearma Seirbhise don tSeirbhis nir a tteighion-se asteach.

D'Fhir Oga aig liostail roimh aois ocht mBliaghna Deag, caithfear an tam do chriochnochadh ocht mBliaghna Deag do chur leis na Seacht, na Deich, no na Dodheag Bliaghna.

As feidir Tearmaighe Serbhise do fhadughadh leis an Oiffigeach ata a Ceomhacht on nGobhernead, Coimhlionaidhe, no Oilean, no Stasun, comhfhad agus bhaineas le Maoir no le Saighdiuraighe a Seirbhis a Muith, go ceann se mhi; agus leis an Riogh, mar bhainios le Maoir no le Saighdiuraighe a Seirbhis a Muith no aig Baile, go Ceann se mhi do Shiothchain gan buairt, tar eis chriochnaithe an Tearma Seirbhise do bhiodar do thabhairt, acht amhain a ccomhnaidhe, nach raghadh an Fadughadh Seirbhise sin an aon Chas, tar thri Bhliaghna.

Aon Mhaor no aon t Saighdiur do liostail air agus ata aig tabhairt a Ttearma Deanaigh Seirbhise, ni cuirfear air bheith a Seirbhis fa'an Ffadughadh Seirbhise sin, acht air feadh se mhi tar eis chriochnaithe an Tearma Denaigh sin.

As feidir Maoir agus Saighdiuraighe do chur as aon Chathlan (Bhattalion) amhain a Ceathlan eile don Regiment cheadna; no ma bhid Crodhfhiothach, a sean Chathlan; acht air a shon sin ni feidir a mbreith as aoin Regiment amhain go Regiment eile gan a ccead fein.

Gach Maor no saighdiur a bfhuil ceart aige air a leigion amach go hiomlan, mas a Muith bhios a Seirbhis an uair sin, do chur don Bhreatain Mhoir no go h'Eirin, saor o Chosdas, agus an Pagha dfaghail do lualtar do Mhaoir agus do Shaighdiuraighe air Mhairsail, on ait a ttiogan se ar tir go ttigh an bParaiste no go ttigh an ait air liostaladh an chead uair e, do reir Dha Mhile Dheag do Mharsail gach aon La, leis na Laethe cinte chum Sgithidh; agus gach aon Mhaor agus Saighdiur a bfhuil ceart ligthe amach aige, do ligfear amach an aon Ait san Rioghacht Aonaigthe, acht amhain an ait duthchais, mar ata reambraite, an Pagha ceadna bheith aige on ait a leigthear air suibhal e go ttigh an ait ar dearbhadh e, mar ta reambraite.

Rataighe Pagha lualtar Pharliament do Mhaoir agus do Shaighdiuraighe an san Arm, aig tosnughadh on 25° La do Juin, 1806, agus an la sin fein.

DRAGUIN GARDA AGUS DRAGUIN.				COISIGHTHE DON LINE CHUM SEIRBHISE CHOITCHEANN.			
	£.	s.	d.		£.	s.	d.
Mor-Mhaor (Serjeant-Major)	0	3	2	Mor-Mhaor no Maor-Maighistir-Cearthamhan	0	1	6
Maor (Serjeant)	0	2	9	Maor	0	1	10
Fodh-Mhaor (Corporal)	0	1	7½	Fodh-Mhaor	0	1	0
An Ceadna tar eis 10 m Bliaghna Seirbhise	0	1	9½	An Ceadna tar eis 7 m Bliaghan Seirbhise	0	1	1
——— 17	0	1	7	Drumaer no Fiofuer	0	1	0
Trumpadoir	0	1	9	Saighdiur	0	1	0
Saighdiur	0	1	4	An Ceadna tar eis 7 m Bliaghan Seirbhise	0	1	1
An Ceadna tar eis 10 m Bliaghna Seirbhise	0	1	5	——— 14			
——— 17							

ORDUIGHTHE AGUS RIAGHLACHA

Bhainios le Maoir agus le Saighdiuraighe do thug a Ttearma cinte Seirbhise, no do leighfear air Siubhal mar Chroilighthigh, Neamhabalta no Loitigthe.

Rata Penstonaidhe Fear do liostail air, agus do leigfear air suibhal tareis tabharthadh a Dara Tearma agus a Ttearma Deanaigh.

MARCSHLUAGH AGUS COISIGHTHE.

				£.	s.	d.
Tar eis an Dara Tearma.						
Mor-Mhaor, Maor-Maighistir-Ceathrabman, Maor, Fodh-Mhaor, agus Saighdiur				0	0	6
Tar eis an Triughadh Tongou.						
Mor-Mhaor, Maor-Maighistir-Ceartbamhan, thug tri Bliaghna a Seirbhis mar sin, an uiriod curtha le an Eiliomh air Pheinsion, mar Mhaor, agus dhcanfas go hiomlan				0	2	0
Maor				0	1	9
Leath-phingin sa lo do chur leis a Scilling san gach Bliaghan seirbhise on Fhodh-Mhaor, agus Pingin air son gach Bliaghan seirbhise na Mhaor, acht na raghaidh an Pension an aon chus tar 1s. 10d.						

Fodh-Mhaor — — — — — — — —
Leath-phingin an lo do chur leis an Scilling ar son gach Bliaghan Seirbhise na Fhodh-Mhaor, acht na raghaidh an Pension an aon chus tar 1s. 6d.
Saighdiur — — — — — — — —

Do Mhor-Mhaoir, do Mhaoir-Maighistire-Cearthamhan, do Mhaoir, d'Fhodh-Mhaoir agus do Shaighdiuraighe a Seirbhis tar eis an Triughadh Tearma, Leathphingin sa lo do chur leis an b Pension air gach Bliaghan Seirbhise tar eis Chriochnaithe an Tearma Deanaigh, gan Teoradh air a Suim.

Saighdiuraighe leigthear air Siubhal roimh Chriochnughadh a Ttearma Seirbhise.

Mhaor no Saighdiur do leigthear air siubhal air feadh an chead Tearma, agus liostalas airis an a Regiment fein, no an aon Regiment eile na ttugthar cead do liostail, lualtar dho coimhriomh, le haghadh eiliomh air Phagha agus Phension, gach Bliaghain do thug se roimhe sin a Seirbhis.

Maor no Saighdiur aig siubhal air feadh an Dara Tearma, lualtar do coimhriomh le Pagha agus le Pension gach Seirbhis roimhe sin, agus aon Bhliaghain air gach da Bhliaghain do bhi as tar eis an Leigion chum Siubhail sin, agus lualtar do Pension Chuig Phinginighe air chriochnughadh an Tearma coimhrimhthe mar sin.

Maor no Saighdiur, leigthe air Suibhal air feadh an triughadh Tearma agus na faghan Pension mar Chrodhligh, mar Loitigh, no Neamhabalta, do gheabhadh se laithreach an Pension as dual do air chriochnughadh an Dara Tearma, agus ionas go faghadh an deisir idir sin agus an Pension is dual do air chriochnughadh an Triughadh Tearma, lualtar do coimhriomh aon Bhliaghan ar son gach da Bhliaghan do bhi se as, tar eis a Leigion air Siubhal, ionas go mbeidh ceart aige air lan Phension aon Sgillinge san lo air chriochnughadh an Triughadh Tearma Coimhrimhthe mar sin.

Saighdiuraighe aig iomeacht air chriochoughadh a Ttearma Seirbhise.

Maor no Saighdiur aig iomeacht as a Seirbhis, agus na dhiagh sin ag dul na Regiment fein, ni choimhriomhadh se le h'iarracht air Bhreis Pagha, an da chead Bhliaghain tar eis na nuadh Listala sin.

Maor no Saighdiur aig iomeacht mar sin, agus ag dul an aon Regiment eile, gan coimhriomh le h'iarracht air Bhreis Pagha, go ceann tri mBlighan tar eis liostala airis mar sin.

Seirbhis an sna Hindiacha Thoir no an sno Hindiacha Thiar.

Maor no Saighdiur, lualtar do coimhriomh tri mBliaghan air gach da Bhliaghain Seirbhise an sna Hindiacha Thoir no Thiar, ionas go mbeidh Eiliomh aige ar Bhreis Pagha agus Pension, ma leigthear air Siubhal .c, acht ni le hagdadh iarracht air a leigion air Siubhal, roimh Crich chinte an Dara Tearma Seirbhise.

Cionas cailtear Breis Pagha agus Pension.

Maoir agus Saighdiuraighe leigthear air Siubhal roimh Chrich a Seirbhise, agus na tig a steach le Riaghlacha agus Orduigthe leactha sios le Commissionairighe Hoisbideil Chelsea aig cur anAimmneacha agus an ait air coimhnaighe aisteach, agus sin do chur a Cceil o Am go hAm, agus na taisbeanan iad fein air Phroclamation an Riogh, no na teid an Gairriosun no a sean Chathlan, ma hiarthar sin ortha le Commissionairighe Hoisbideil Chealsea, caillid gach aon cheart air Bhreis Pagha, no air Phension, a riocht Seirbhise; acht ni feidir gloadh air aon t Saighdiur chum na Seirbhise sin, fa aon Phroclamation no Pha aon Ordugha o Chommissionairighe Hoisbideil Chelsea, do thug go hiomlan a Thri Ttearmaidhe Seirbhise, do reir na Riaghlacha so.

As feidir a Pagha go leir no aon Chuid de, aon Eiliomh air Bhreis Pagha no Pension, air son Bliaghan Seirbhise roimhe, do bhaint do Mhaor agus do Shaighdiur le Breith Choitean Comhairle Cogaidh, (Sentence of a General Court Martial.)

Rataidhe Pensionaidhe Maor agus Saighdiuraighe leigthe air Siubhal, air bheith neamh abalta no neamh-etriomhnach chum Seirbhise.

			£.	s.	d.
Ma taid neamhabalta air ambeatha do thoilleamhuin			0	1	3
Ma taid neamhabalta acht ionamhail le ni eigin do thoilleamhuin le na mbeathughadh			0	1	1
Ma taid lag acht abalta air mbuith mhor doibh fein			0	0	9
Ma taid gan bheith abalta air Seirbhis acht abalta air a mbeatha do thoilleamhuin			0	0	6
Caithfeadh na Fir do bheadh, as le a neamhabaltacht amhain, an aon don da Eagar deirionach, madh radhgair air Suibhal iad air feadh an Triughadh Tearma, Pension aon Sgillinge dfaghail.					

Ni lualtar do Mhaor na do Shaighdiur, iarracht do reir Cirt air aon Phension don tsort so, ma thig a Neamhabaltacht no Neamhoireamhnacht do dhruim Lochta no Mio-mhacnais.

Aig Commissionairighe Chelsea ata Ordughadh cidh an tEagar Pensin ambainean gach aon Fhear leis, agus ata Comhacht aca aistriughadh as Eagar amhain go h'Eagar eile.

As feidir leis na Commissionairighe glaodh airis air Mhaoir no air Shaighdiuraighe da lualtar Pension don t'sort sin, no go ccriochnaid a Ttearma Seirbhise.

Caithfear na Horduighthe agus na Riaghlacha reambraite do thuigsin mar bhainid leis na Maoir agus leis na Saighdiuraighe amhain do liostail tar eis an 24d la don June so chuaidh thoruin; acht ata ceart aig Maoir agus aig Saighdiuraighe do liostaladh roimhe sin (chum Seirbhise choitean) ar son a roimh Seirbhise Lan Luail agus Maith a bfhuil an so curtha sios, an gach a mbainion le Pagha agus le Luaidhiocht agus le Pensionaighe, ma leigthear air suibhal iad mar Chroilightigh, Neamhabalta no Loitigthe, no tar eis Tearma Seirbhise nach lugha na Cheithre Bliaghna Deug.

CURTHA A CCLODH LE ABRAM BRAIDLIGH KING, STAISIONOIR MHORDHACHT AN RIOGH AIG UIMHIR 36, A SRAID NA BAINTIAGHARNA, DA NGOIRTHEAR A SAGSBHEARLA, DAME-STREET, A MBAILEATHA-CLIATH.

16 A proclamation issued by the War Office, a branch of the Chief Secretary's Office in Dublin Castle, 1806. (70 x 57 cm.)

The proclamation is an Irish version of the published 'Rules and Regulations for the Better Ordering of His Majesty's Army', which outlined the conditions of service and the rates of pay and pensions in the regular army. This version was for recruiting purposes in Irish-speaking areas and 5,000 copies were printed; at the time there were at least three and a half million Irish speakers but relatively few could read the language. In any case, recruiting must have been effective as it has been estimated that over 75,000 Irishmen joined the British army between 1805 and 1815, mainly for service in the Napoleonic Wars. Indeed, the Irish element in Wellington's armies contributed significantly to his victories. More than one person may have been involved in the translation of the document as it has elements of both Munster and Connacht Irish. The Library has two copies of the proclamation, both donated.

War-Office, October 22, 1806.
RULES AND REGULATIONS
For the better ordering of His Majesty's Army, and for improving the Condition of Soldiers, as contained in His Majesty's Warrant of the 7th October 1806, and in certain Acts passed during the last Session of Parliament.

Periods and Terms of Inlisting.

In the Infantry —	7 Years.
Cavalry —	10 do.
Artillery —	12 do.

Men willing to engage for a Second Period of Service, will be re-inlisted.

In the Infantry, for —	7 Years.
Cavalry —	7 do.
Artillery —	5 do.

Men willing to engage for a Third Period of Service, will be re-inlisted.

In the Infantry, for —	7 Years.
Cavalry —	7 do.
Artillery —	5 do.

Extract from *The Dublin Gazette*, 30 October 1806.

Police  Gazette,

OR

HUE-AND-CRY.

Published for Ireland on every Tuesday and Friday.

All Notices intended for insertion in the Hue-and-Cry, are to be transmitted under cover addressed to the Inspector-General of Constabulary (the words Hue-and-Cry to be written on the left hand corner of the Envelope). No Description can be inserted unless an Information shall have been Sworn; but it is not necessary to forward the Informations to the Inspector-General.

As the Law (48 Geo. 3, c. 140, s. 44,) only permits the insertion of Notices respecting Felonies, no other description of Notice can be inserted in the Hue-and-Cry.

DUBLIN, TUESDAY, NOVEMBER 28, 1865.

By the Lord Lieutenant-General and General Governor of Ireland.

A PROCLAMATION.

WODEHOUSE.

WHEREAS, *James Stephens*, has been an active Member of a Treasonable Conspiracy against the Queen's authority in *Ireland*, and has this Morning escaped from the *Richmond Prison*.

NOW WE, being determined to bring the said *James Stephens* to Justice, Do hereby offer a Reward of

ONE THOUSAND POUNDS

to any person or persons who shall give such information as shall lead to the Arrest of the said *James Stephens*.

AND WE do hereby offer a further Reward of

THREE HUNDRED POUNDS

to any Person or Persons who shall give such information as shall lead to the Arrest of any one whomsoever who has knowingly harboured or received, or concealed, or assisted or aided in any way whatsoever in his Escape from Arrest, the said *James Stephens*

And We do also hereby offer a FREE PARDON, in addition to the above-mentioned REWARD, to any Person or Persons concerned in the Escape of the said JAMES STEPHENS who shall give such Information as shall lead to his Arrest as aforesaid.

Given at Her Majesty's Castle of *Dublin*, this *Twenty-fourth* day of *November*, 1865.

By His Excellency's Command,

THOS. A. LARCOM.

Description of the above-named JAMES STEPHENS:—

JAMES STEPHENS is about 42 years of age; 5 feet 7 inches high; stout make; broad high shoulders; very tight active appearance; fair hair, bald all round top of head, wears all his beard, which is sandy, slightly tinged with grey, rather long under the chin, but slight round the jaw approaching the ears; broad forehead; tender eyes, which defect seems to be constitutional, and has a peculiar habit of closing the left eye when speaking; high cheek bones, and rather good looking countenance; hands and feet remarkably small and well formed, and he generally dresses in black clothes.

James Stephens,
from a contemporary woodcut.

17 *The Police Gazette,* Dublin, file 1843-1893.

The Police Gazette was an official publication issued by Dublin Castle two or three
times a week and distributed to police barracks and various officials throughout the
country. It included information on law and order and on crime; it also gave details
of escaped convicts, army deserters and missing persons. The issue shown here
included a 'wanted' notice for James Stephens, the Fenian leader, who had just
escaped from Richmond Bridewell (afterwards Griffith Barracks and now Griffith
College). The notice appeared for a considerable period but without result –
Stephens escaped to Paris and from there to New York.

The proclamation was issued by the Under-Secretary, Thomas Larcom, at the
direction of the Lord Lieutenant, Lord Wodehouse. Larcom is best remembered for
his contributions earlier on with the Ordnance Survey and the Board of Works;
Wodehouse was noted for his strong measures against the Fenians.

18 The 1916 Proclamation. (76 x 51 cm.)

The proclamation was composed mainly by Patrick Pearse, and was approved by the Military Council of the Irish Republican Brotherhood. It is probable that six of the signatories signed the manuscript early in Holy Week at a meeting in Mrs Jennie Wyse Power's house at 21 Henry Street. Joseph Mary Plunkett was then in a nursing home and signed later. The printing was done on an old Wharfdale printing press in Liberty Hall early on Easter Sunday, 23 April. There was not enough type to print the whole document so the top half was printed first; the type was then re-set to print the lower half. This accounts for the different density of the two halves. The number of copies printed was 2,500; the reason for the seemingly large number was that it was intended that copies would be distributed throughout the country.

At noon on Easter Monday, immediately after the occupation of the General Post Office, Pearse came out onto the street and read the proclamation. Seán T. O'Kelly (who at one time worked in the National Library) was given charge of distribution, and copies were posted up around the city centre.

Liberty Hall; it was shelled by the gunboat *Helga* during Easter Week.

POBLACHT NA H EIREANN.

THE PROVISIONAL GOVERNMENT

OF THE

IRISH REPUBLIC

TO THE PEOPLE OF IRELAND.

IRISHMEN AND IRISHWOMEN : In the name of God and of the dead generations from which she receives her old tradition of nationhood, Ireland, through us, summons her children to her flag and strikes for her freedom.

Having organised and trained her manhood through her secret revolutionary organisation, the Irish Republican Brotherhood, and through her open military organisations, the Irish Volunteers and the Irish Citizen Army, having patiently perfected her discipline, having resolutely waited for the right moment to reveal itself, she now seizes that moment, and, supported by her exiled children in America and by gallant allies in Europe, but relying in the first on her own strength, she strikes in full confidence of victory.

We declare the right of the people of Ireland to the ownership of Ireland, and to the unfettered control of Irish destinies, to be sovereign and indefeasible. The long usurpation of that right by a foreign people and government has not extinguished the right, nor can it ever be extinguished except by the destruction of the Irish people. In every generation the Irish people have asserted their right to national freedom and sovereignty; six times during the past three hundred years they have asserted it in arms. Standing on that fundamental right and again asserting it in arms in the face of the world, we hereby proclaim the Irish Republic as a Sovereign Independent State, and we pledge our lives and the lives of our comrades-in-arms to the cause of its freedom, of its welfare, and of its exaltation among the nations.

The Irish Republic is entitled to, and hereby claims, the allegiance of every Irishman and Irishwoman. The Republic guarantees religious and civil liberty, equal rights and equal opportunities to all its citizens, and declares its resolve to pursue the happiness and prosperity of the whole nation and of all its parts, cherishing all the children of the nation equally, and oblivious of the differences carefully fostered by an alien government, which have divided a minority from the majority in the past.

Until our arms have brought the opportune moment for the establishment of a permanent National Government, representative of the whole people of Ireland and elected by the suffrages of all her men and women, the Provisional Government, hereby constituted, will administer the civil and military affairs of the Republic in trust for the people.

We place the cause of the Irish Republic under the protection of the Most High God, Whose blessing we invoke upon our arms, and we pray that no one who serves that cause will dishonour it by cowardice, inhumanity, or rapine. In this supreme hour the Irish nation must, by its valour and discipline and by the readiness of its children to sacrifice themselves for the common good, prove itself worthy of the august destiny to which it is called.

Signed on Behalf of the Provisional Government,

THOMAS J. CLARKE,

SEAN Mac DIARMADA,   THOMAS MacDONAGH,
P. H. PEARSE,   EAMONN CEANNT,
JAMES CONNOLLY.   JOSEPH PLUNKETT.

III. POSTERS, BROADSIDES, BALLADS

In recent decades there has been a growing interest in social history and people generally are becoming increasingly curious about the way of life of former generations. A major source for this type of information is ephemeral publicity documentation such as notices and posters which were addressed to the public at large and displayed wherever people gathered. They were often concerned with the serious issues of the day, for instance, land, landlords and politics, or with leisure pursuits such as sport and entertainment. They indicate the preoccupations of people at particular times in the past, and they suggest that we are really not very different from our ancestors, though our circumstances have utterly changed.

The National Library has accumulated considerable quantities of this type of ephemeral material. It is difficult to be precise about the numbers as many of the items have not been centralised but are kept as part of the collections with which they were acquired, for instance collections of estate papers. In addition to such holdings which can be traced through the main catalogues, the Library has developed a specific collection of posters and broadsides which amounts to about 4,000 items. This has been built up over the years and includes items acquired with the RDS Library, items from the E.R. McClintock Dix Collection donated in the early decades of the century, and various other items received by purchase or donation over the years. For many years the Library has also solicited this type of material directly from the originating bodies, especially theatres and political parties.

Generally, this type of publicity item has a very short life, and if it is not acquired within a week or two of production it may be lost forever. Or, years later, a copy may turn up in a bookseller's catalogue and one has to pay, perhaps, hundreds of pounds for an item which could once have been picked up free of charge. The history of this type of publication is ancient and attested from classical times, but it is only with the development of printing and mass-production in the fifteenth century that it became common. Governments and civil authorities used the medium in official proclamations, and gradually the technique was adopted by anybody with a message or product to promote. In times long before television or radio and when newspapers were the preserve of an affluent minority, posters and broadsides were a means of mass communication, providing a cheap and readily available medium for informing and influencing the general public. They were designed to inform, attract, persuade and convince, and were usually couched in emotive, colourful and powerful language.

Such strong language is typical of the many items in the Library's collection emanating from Daniel O'Connell's campaigns for Catholic Emancipation and Repeal of the Union. This style and tradition continued through the

Land War and Home Rule agitation and has survived into contemporary political propaganda.

The poster format came into its own in the last decades of the nineteenth century, with improvements in printing technology which culminated in the full-colour poster. The 1914-18 War was the occasion for an intensive and imaginative poster campaign by the British authorities, and the Library has a good collection of specimens. The focus changed at various stages, ranging from War Loan subscriptions to recruitment and on to aid for widows, orphans and refugees. The campaign for recruits increasingly resorted to moral pressure. Typically, the message was terse and emotive, for instance, 'Irishmen – Avenge the Lusitania', or Kitchener's famous 'Your Country Needs You'. The announcement of conscription in Britain prompted the Anti-Conscription Pledge, 5,000 copies of which mushroomed, as if by magic, overnight in Dublin – a response by poster to an official proclamation. The 1916-21 conflict was also the source of a rich harvest for the National Library. For instance, there is the handbill issued by James Connolly's *Worker's Republic* on the Saturday before the Rising announcing, 'Liberty Hall salutes the Sunburst of Ireland'. From the Civil War period the propaganda campaign for the hearts and minds of the people is graphically represented with allegation and counter-allegation in poster and bulletin.

On the return to normality, the focus turned back to goods and services. With the advent of cinema, glossy publicity materials produced by foreign film studios boosted Irish standards in design and presentation, and increasingly publicity and advertising brochures were generated by specialised commercial agencies. Outside of Dublin, however, the promoters of sports, carnivals, dances, auctions or politics generally relied on the local printers. These traditional craftsmen could be relied on to communicate the required message to good effect by judiciously exploiting their often limited range of type. A recent acquisition, the Liam O'Leary Film Archives, is particularly interesting in that it includes posters not only from Holywood, London, Rome and Berlin but also from many towns around the country, and is a valuable source for the history of design in the twentieth century.

The Library also has a collection of over 3,000 nineteenth-century broadside ballads which are similar in some respects to the popular posters of the period. They are usually anonymous and roughly printed on one side of a sheet of cheap paper, generally with a crude woodcut decoration which is not always pertinent to the subject. They were often composed by hack poets commissioned by the local printer; the market was considerable and a popular ballad could sometimes save a printer from bankruptcy. The themes tend to be of occasional or local interest and include sport, love and tragedy. A high percentage reflect an obsession with oppression and rebellion, be the obsession that of the composer or the market. The broadsides were bought and hawked around the streets and at fairs and markets by professional ballad-singers, some of whom were illiterate. Over thirty of the ballads are wholly or partly in Irish, including a number collected by Thomas Davis who died in 1845. They are printed in roman script and rendered according to the conventions of English spelling. While the majority of people spoke Irish, few could read it, and this style of presentation made the ballads more generally intelligible. Like various other manifestations of folk art and popular culture, these posters, broadsides and ballads which were once ubiquitous are now rare or unique and may well be regarded as treasures.

'The Irish emigrant outward bound ', Berlin, *c.* 1850.

A LEMENTATION ON THE
Parish of Anaghdown.

6

Daun sva slanta veith cauht aer go bragh,
Er a meid sht baihn uin Annagh Cloon,
Laih cho bra leish—gon gee na basthee,
Laun O waud ochu thuggoo er sool ;
Vei na fir gelistoch clei agus keitock,
Trevoh creare agus craihu sheeul,
Na marah ya yrear shin enough da chean nes,
Snefuh breideen agus anrut cheeul.

If I had help there would be tald made,
Of all those drowned in Annagh Cloon,
Such a fine day without rain or wind,
Th» full of the boat was whipt away,
There was some men would plough and harrow,
That would shake the seed and go through the land
Besides some women that would net and freize,
And not foregetting the linen too.

Thulla kleva agus loskn sleva,
Er a naut sho hraig muid agus molam creigh,
A leightee cretoor dan shea fein laig,
Nei deevaul oleis chor a dror yum,
Augh mea mor er a Guslaun Noo,
Do vaa creaghun an chora gura banu mor an
Daigee O dolaus er Annagh Cloon.

A wara nes Ruane a chaleen sperule,
Ish thu an Van bo glesthee a vee ansa maud,
Dhimmy thu vuim sa a maquin kedin,
Gol o necoy go Cruck o Dullane,
Do vei turkey red orhee ga hou an edhes,
Cappeen lace agus ribbeen baun ;
Agus gor og thu do vaurheen shier thmin grothee,
Guil na nor go trum do yeigo.

A Shaun O Cosgroch ma kuig keid slan lath,
Be thu an mac a bar do vei eg Ban O rier,
Dimmy thu veim sa a muigh de kedeen,
Agus thu gui neeny go Cruck O Dhullane ;
Heilh do varheen da maithe kead farh
Go dbura an sway lata O thu O snav ;
Augh quig keid hannacht lath,
Gar corth na glore ler do shrrim ga flaihus Dheia.

Dheiry mea hein ga mach Dhehina,
Choola mea an keenu agus an gradu bus—
Eg na mra trum tursogh da var na heeagh,
Gon koe deeou augh a sheen curpe ;
Brishy band agus seop ue deeneigh,
Agus thugoo na na keeree mach as any snay,
Gor thugu u walla eid agus go narau asheenu,
Mor ein nar deig an agus ochtae mra.

As I got up of a Friday morning,
I heard the crying and the clapping hauds,
Of all those women tired and weary,
And nothing to do but stuitching crops.
The boat was broke and the christians scattered,
And the Lord have mercy all on their souls,
For now to count you up the number—
There was eight women, and eleven men.

19 A broadside ballad with part of **'Anach Cuain',** early nineteenth century.

'Anach Cuain', composed by Antoine Raifteirí (c.1784–1835), the blind poet and fiddler, commemorates a tragic boating accident on Lough Corrib, Co. Galway in September 1828. Thirty-one people were travelling with livestock in an old currach from Anaghdown near Headford to a fair in Galway, when a sheep put a foot through the bottom. In the panic, the boat capsized and eleven women and eight men were drowned. Raifteirí's lament was probably composed soon after; it is likely that the ballad was published while the tragedy was fresh in people's minds.

Some of the text is in Irish, but as few people could read the language the words were spelled as if they were English. The first two lines are a rendering of, *Dá bhfaighinnse sláinte bheadh caint air go brách/Ar an méid a bádh in Eanach Dhúin.* An English version begins at line ten; the use of both languages was intended to broaden the appeal and the market.
The woodcut at the head shows a sea-going brigantine of a type built at Leitir Mealláin (Lettermullan), Co. Galway, and which traded between Ireland and North America. The printer probably had the woodcut for use in advertising passage on such ships, and used it here for want of something more specific.

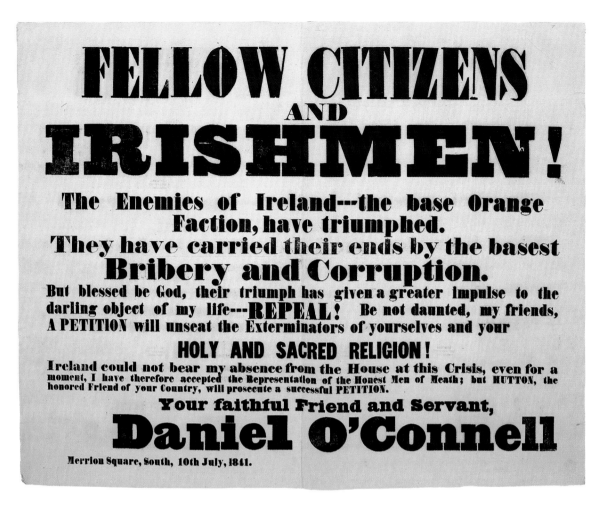

20 A poster issued by **Daniel O'Connell and the Repeal Association** after the July 1841 general election. (46 x 58 cm.)

The Repeal Association was founded by Daniel O'Connell on 15 April 1840 to promote the repeal of the Act of Union of 1800 and the restoration of an Irish parliament. In the contest for the City of Dublin in the 1841 general election, O'Connell and the Liberal candidate, Robert Hutton, were defeated by the Tory candidates, John Beatty West and Edmund Grogan. The nationalist press accused the Dublin Corporation officials, especially the sheriff, Joshua Porter, of malpractice, and O'Connell considered petitioning Parliament to have the result overturned. His seat in Parliament was, however, assured as he was returned for Meath, as mentioned in the poster, and also for Cork County which he eventually chose to represent. As it transpired the proposed petition never materialised.

The tone of the poster is typical of the period. It was issued from O'Connell's Dublin house at 30 Merrion Square, South.

21 A notice issued by Sir Charles Domvile, 18 May 1864.

Sir Charles Domvile owned 6,000 acres of land in Co. Dublin, and was one of the many landlords who, on occasion, communicated with staff, tenants and the general public through the medium of printed notices. The family came to Ireland at the beginning of the seventeenth century; in 1660 Sir William Domvile was appointed Attorney-General by Charles II, and was granted an estate at Loughlinstown in South County Dublin. The family later acquired lands at Templeogue (also in South Dublin) and at Santry, to the north of the City. The Domvile estate records, acquired by the Library in the 1950s, provide detailed information on the management of a typical landed estate. Various printed notices in the collection indicate unequivocally the relationship between master and servant as seen by a fairly typical landlord of the period.

Santry House, a lithograph from a drawing by Lady Domvile, Sir Charles' mother.

I REQUIRE every Labourer to keep his Clothes clean and well mended, and to wear Laced Boots, Leather Gaiters to his knee.

Corduroy Breeches and Waistcoat, Neck Tie and Smock Frock, with Black Felt Hat.

I expect that any small Repairs his Cottage, &c., may require, he will himself make, such as nailing a Rail, or colouring a Breach in the Plaister, or repairing a Pane of Glass.

And also that he will keep his Garden, Cottage, Offices, &c., and the road along his Garden, or out-side the Gate he has charge of, clean.

It is his duty to prevent any one, whether in my service or not, damaging my property, ill-using my animals, making short cuts, taking things, out of their places, and to let me know as soon as possible.

His whole time being mine, he is not to leave home without permission, as each man is liable to be called in at night, in case of fire, &c.

CHARLES DOMVILE.

Santry House,
18th May, 1864.

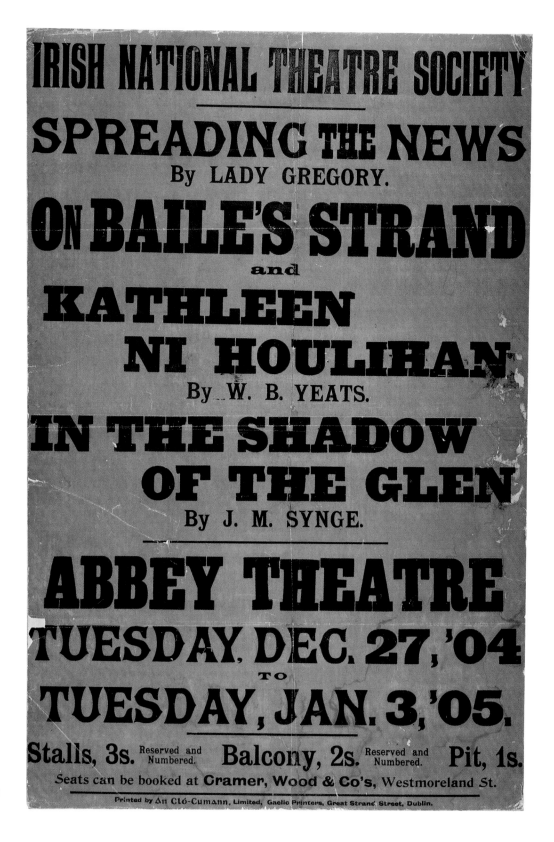

58

22 The poster for the opening of the Abbey Theatre on 27 December 1904.
(75 x 50 cm.)

The Abbey Theatre was established by the merger of the Irish Literary Theatre
(founded by W.B. Yeats, Edward Martyn and Lady Gregory) and W.G. Fay's Irish
National Dramatic Society. The building, the former Mechanics' Institute in Abbey
Street, was provided by Annie Fredericka Horniman, an English patron of the arts.
   The poster was acquired with the large collection of theatre memorabilia and
diaries donated by Joseph Holloway, the architect who renovated the building.
Holloway was an inveterate attender of first-nights; he was present on the opening
night and his diary gives an account of the proceedings. Many notabilities were
present, including John Dillon, John Redmond, Hugh Lane and John Masefield.
Holloway's diary records: 'The night was memorable and the house was thronged
and genuinely enthusiastic'.

NO. 1. THIRD YEAR

A BROADSIDE

FOR JUNE, 1910
PUBLISHED MONTHLY BY E. C. YEATS AT THE CUALA PRESS,
CHURCHTOWN, DUNDRUM, COUNTY DUBLIN.
SUBSCRIPTION TWELVE SHILLINGS A YEAR POST FREE.

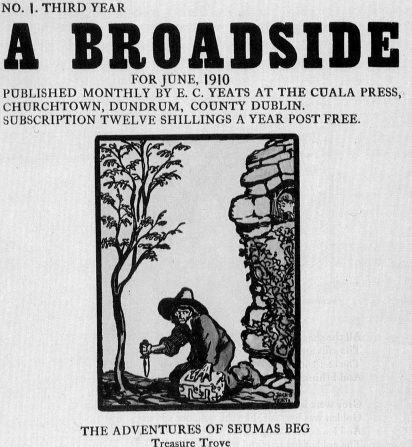

THE ADVENTURES OF SEUMAS BEG
Treasure Trove

His arms were round the box. It was of wood
Clamped strong with bands of iron and it seemed
To be an awful weight. At last he stood,
And I stole closer still. His white eyes gleamed
As he peeped here and there and then he laid
The box down on the ground. A knife he drew
Out from his pocket and he plunged the blade
Deep down into the ground: the clay soon flew
In all directions underneath a tree.
And when the hole was deep he buried low
The box, and filled the hole again, and cunningly,
Stamped all the soil down flat. I went next day
To dig the treasure up but lost my way.

James Stephens.

300 copies only.

23 A Cuala Press *Broadside,* June 1910. (28 x 19 cm.)

The Cuala Press, originally the Dun Emer Press, was founded in 1908 by Elizabeth Corbet Yeats and her sister Susan Mary ('Lollie' and 'Lily') and named after the local barony. In the period 1908-15 it issued a series of four-page broadsides, illustrated by Jack Butler Yeats (their brother). The broadsides were hand coloured by various people, including Eileen Colum, a sister of Padraic Colum. The Library has the complete series and also a later series published in the thirties.

The series was inspired by the traditional broadside ballads which were still common at the time. It featured some of the best of the old ballads and also poems by such well-known contemporary writers as Padraic Colum, John Masefield and W. B. Yeats. In addition to his drawings, Jack B. Yeats contributed a number of poems to the series, some anonymous and some signed with his pseudonyms, 'R.E. MacGowan' and 'Wolfe Tone MacGowan'. James Stephens (1880-1950) was a frequent contributor; he is now remembered for his substantial corpus of lyric poetry and for his novels, especially *The Charwoman's Daughter* and *The Crock of Gold,* both of which were published in 1912.

Elizabeth Corbet Yeats working the printing press at Dun Emer, *c.* 1904.

24 A poster issued by Conradh na Gaeilge in 1917 for its annual Hallowe'en festival, Féile na Samhna. (89 x 57 cm.)

Conradh na Gaeilge was founded in July 1893 as the Gaelic League. Its main aims were the revival and preservation of the Irish language and traditional Irish culture. It organised Irish classes and various other cultural activities including Féile na Samhna. In 1917 the main events of the festival were a concert featuring notable musicians and singers and a céilí, both held in the Mansion House. The Conradh newspaper, *An Claidheamh Soluis,* reported on the concert in its issue of 10 November 1917 and a paragraph is reproduced here.

The attractive design features the arms of the four provinces, reflecting the desire of An Conradh to unite all Irishmen through their common nationality. The poster was printed from art-work by a lithographic process; the printing was done by the Dublin firm of O'Loughlin, Murphy and Boland (rendered in Irish on the poster). John O'Loughlin's son, Colm Ó Lochlainn, was afterwards proprietor of the well-known press, The Sign of the Three Candles.

Iad So Léir !

Má deineamair tagairt fé leit de Mairsile isé ba cúis leis ná gur dóig linn gurab í seo an céad uair aici ag teacht go Baile Áta Cliat chun amráin do gabáil ag cuirm ccóil móir—gur duine "nuad" i i gcúrsaib amránaid- eact agus duine go "gcloisfar uaiti" arís. Ac ní fágann son ná gur tuill na daoine eile árdmolad com mait céadna. Tá an oiread son díob ann ná fuil sé de flige aguinn tagairt fé leit a déanam do gac duine do tuill é. Níl aguinn le déanam ac a rád gur mór an molad do tuill Dubglas Frinseac Ó Maolám, Máire Daimgin, Próinsias Ó Súilliobáin, Séamus Clandiolún, Art Ó Darlaig, Treasa Mc Cormaic, Seán Ó Naoisín, Gearóid Crofta, Pól Ó Feargail agus Tomás Ramsam.

63

64

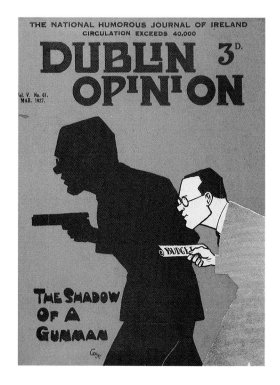

25 A poster issued by Cumann na nGaedheal for the 1932 or the 1933 general election. (76 x 50 cm.)

Traditionally, Cumann na nGaedheal presented itself as the party of law and order. In this period it made much of the fact that it had taken exceptionally restrictive measures against the I.R.A. in October 1931. Here, it used the title of the popular O'Casey play, *The Shadow of a Gunman* (1923), to promote its own image and to associate De Valera and Fianna Fáil, the main opposition, with the use of force. It possibly echoes the cover of *Dublin Opinion* from March 1927 which featured the Minister for Finance, Ernest Blythe.

In the 1927 and subsequent elections, Cumann na nGaedheal mounted extremely professional advertising campaigns, which were organised with the help of the Dublin agency, O'Kennedy & Brindley (as it was then named). In the event, while returned to power in the two 1927 elections, Cumann na nGaedheal was defeated in 1932 and 1933.

THROUGH FIRE AND WATER

FILM DIRECTOR: ALEXANDER ROU
FEATURING:
NATALIYA SEDYKH

GEORGI MILLYAR

SOVEXPORTFILM

26 A poster for the English version of the Russian film, ***Through Fire and Water,*** 1968. (109 x 84 cm.)

This was one of many children's films by the talented director, Alexander Arthurovitch Rowe (1906-73), the son of a milling expert from Co. Wexford and a Greek mother. Rowe was a pioneer of the Soviet film industry; in recognition of his contribution over many years, he was made an Honoured Artist of the Soviet Republics.

This is one of the many striking posters in the Liam O'Leary Film Archives which were generously presented to the Library in 1986.

Liam O'Leary.

IV. NEWSPAPERS

The newspaper collection is one of the National Library's most important resources. It is especially significant in that it is the largest collection of Irish newspapers in the country and is the focus for researchers from all parts of Ireland. It consists mainly of newspapers of Irish interest, and it includes complete files of a high percentage of the several hundred titles which have been published from the late seventeenth century to the present day. In addition to the mainstream national and provincial newspapers, there are specialist organs devoted to matters such as sport, agriculture or politics, papers published in Irish centres abroad, and, mainly from recent years, a number of free commercial advertisers. At the present time the Library receives over three hundred newspapers, that is, it receives and files each issue, be it daily or weekly of that number of titles.

In common with most of the other National Library collections, the newspaper collection originated in the RDS Library which by 1877 had substantial holdings. The Joly Library also had some important material, especially files of early short-run Irish newspapers and foreign news-sheets. From the beginning, it was National Library policy to acquire all current Irish newspapers, provincial as well as national, but it did not have adequate funds at its disposal. The difficulty was not as acute as it might have been however, as many of the newspaper proprietors sent on their papers free of charge according as they were published. In addition, various institutions and societies which took current newspapers and periodicals for the use of staff or members afterwards passed them on to the National Library. By 1900 the Library was receiving some forty newspapers and journals presented by publishers and institutions. In its early days the Library also received many donations of back files.

A particularly welcome windfall came in 1922 from what might hardly have been regarded as a likely source – the Chief Secretary's Office in Dublin Castle. It consisted of 4,000 volumes, including extensive files of many provincial titles accumulated by the Office over the years as a source of information on political or subversive activity around the country. In recent decades, the Library has filled many gaps in the collection by acquiring microfilm copies of eighteenth- and nineteenth-century files from the British Museum Library (now the British Library) which has very comprehensive holdings of Irish newspapers. Following copyright legislation in 1927, the acquisition of newspapers and periodicals became more systematic, and most of those published in the Republic have since been acquired free of charge. Newspapers and periodicals published in Northern Ireland are not covered by Irish copyright law, but these are also acquired either by donation or purchase.

The first long-run newspapers appeared in the eighteenth century. Among the more important were three provincial titles which have survived to the present day: the *(Belfast) News-Letter* (1737-), *The Limerick Chronicle* (1766-), and the *(London) Derry Journal* (1772-). Among the more notable of the national newspapers were *Faulkner's Dublin Journal*, *Saunder's Newsletter*, and, in particular, *The Freeman's Journal* (1763-1924) which was generally popular and nationalist in its sympathies.

Eighteenth-century newspapers were much more limited in their coverage than modern papers and the presentation of news items was extremely terse and in the manner of a bulletin. Their focus was generally on Britain rather than Ireland and local events received scant coverage. They included dispatches of British and foreign news, and the doings of royalty and aristocracy received a disproportionate amount of space. A general feature, however, which makes them a fruitful source for the social historian is that they tended to carry a good deal of advertising, both official and commercial. Overall, despite their shortcomings, eighteenth-century newspapers constitute a major resource for those studying the political, economic and social history of the period.

In the course of the nineteenth century the newspaper industry expanded very considerably. It flourished in most parts of the country but particularly in Ulster, especially around Belfast which was then the most industrialised city in Ireland. Among the contributory factors were the development of reel paper and mechanised printing presses which reduced costs for the proprietors and eventually for the readers. Another factor was the removal of stamp duty on most newspapers in the 1850s. A general lowering in costs coincided with the growth in literacy in the decades after the establishment of the national school system in the 1830s. With advances in technology, the design and layout became more attractive and some papers included illustrations. Professional reporters provided more extensive coverage of local news, and many newspapers had some literary content.

An interesting feature of nineteenth-century newspaper publishing is the large number of political papers. Among these were *The Pilot*, published by Daniel O'Connell; the influential Young Ireland paper, *The Nation;* and the Fenian paper, *The Irish People*. In the 1880s, the most notable of the political organs were *United Ireland*, representing the Land League and Home Rule movements, and *The Union* which spoke for the landlords. An important development towards the end of the nineteenth century was the appearance of newspapers in the Irish language. The most notable was *An Claidheamh Soluis* which was published by the Gaelic League and first appeared in 1898.

The physical management of such large numbers of newspapers has special problems. The newspapers are bound in hard covers and shelved like books, but long-term preservation is difficult, especially in the case of those published since the middle of the last century. These are printed on paper made from wood-pulp which has a high acid content and tends to discolour and disintegrate with age. To minimise handling and to preserve the information many of them have been microfilmed. The Library is also involved in the inter-library NEWSPLAN project which is establishing priorities for the microfilming and conservation of newspapers. Increasingly in the future, newspapers will be made available to readers on microfilm or some other medium rather than in hardcopy.

As well as being one of the largest collections in the National Library, the newspaper collection is one of the most heavily used. As a major source for political and social studies at national and local levels, it attracts professional researchers and casual enquirers with an almost infinite variety of interests.

The cover of a National Library publication, 1983.

An Account of the chief
OCCURRENCES
OF IRELAND;
Together with some Particulars from
ENGLAND:

From Wednesday the 15 *of* Febr. *to Wednesday* 22 *of* February.

February the 15. 1659.

His day closed with the happy miscarriage of a design intended against Sir *Ch. Coote* L. President of *Connaught*, Sir *Theophilus Iones*, and other faithfull Officers of the Army, which was thought by some to be so securely laid, and so ripened in time, that there wanted nothing but execution. The history thereof may be thus calculated and contracted, *viz.*

The Army having by their Declaration on the 14 of *December* last, declared against the sinfull interruptions put on the Parliament, thought it their duty thoroughly to pursue the ends of that Engagement; and finding the interruption given the Parliament in 1648, to be owned and justified by those now sitting, thought themselves bound in duty to declare for the secluded Members : for prevention whereof, some fanatick spirits prevailed with Sir *Hardress Waller* to remove the Convention of Officers appointed at the Custom-house (their usual place of their Meeting) to the Castle, which they knew being better fortified with Guns than Reasons, was the more likely to give success to their intended Design of surprising the said Sir

A *Charls*

RAPIN's
HISTORY OF ENGLAND.

CHARLES THE SECOND.

Published by M. Fletcher, &c.......Price London 1835.

27 *An Account of the Chief Occurrences,* Dublin, 1660. (18 x 15 cm.)

This is generally regarded as the first newspaper published in Ireland. It was published weekly and at least five issues appeared; each issue consisted of four pages. The first two issues were acquired by the Library in 1934 and it has facsimile copies of the others. This issue of the paper was published in February 1660; according to the calendar of the period (Old Style) the year began on 25 March (Lady Day) and the period 1 January to 24 March was dated as the previous year.

It was published by Sir Charles Coote whose father came over with Lord Mountjoy in 1600. Sir Charles held high office under Cromwell's government, but changed sides and at this stage supported Charles II whose fortunes were in the ascendant. The newspaper was designed to promote the Restoration; the first issue describes a struggle between Coote and anti-Restoration forces under Sir Hardress Waller ('some fanatic spirits') for control of Dublin Castle. Sir Charles was created Earl of Mountrath for his efforts on behalf of the Restoration. The Cootes acquired confiscated O'Reilly lands in Co. Cavan and gave their name to the town of Cootehill.

THE NATION.

" To create and to foster public opinion in Ireland—to make it racy of the soil."—CHIEF BARON WOULFE.

DUBLIN, SATURDAY, OCTOBER 15, 1842.

THE NATION.

With all the nicknames that serve to delude and divide us—with all their Orangemen and Ribbonmen, Torymen and Whigmen, Ultras and Moderados, and Heaven knows what rubbish besides, there are, in truth, but two parties in Ireland : those who suffer from her National degradation, and those who profit by it. To a country like ours, all other distinctions are unimportant. This is the first article of our political creed; and as we desire to be known for what we are, we make it our earliest task to announce that the object of the writers of this journal is to organise the greater and better of those parties, and to strive, with all our soul and with all our strength, for the diffusion and establishment of its principles. This will be the beginning, middle, and end of our labours.

And we come to the task with a strong conviction that there never was a moment more favorable for such a purpose than the present. The old parties are broken, or breaking up, both in England and Ireland—Whiggery, which never had a soul, has now no body; and the simplest partisan, or the most selfish expectant—who is generally a creature quite as unreasonable—cannot ask us to fix the hopes of our country on the fortunes of a party so weak and fallen. Far less can we expect anything from Toryism, which could only serve us by ceasing *to be* Toryism ; even in its new and modified form it means the identical reverse of all we require to make the masses in this country happier and better. But this shifting of parties—this loosening of belief in old distinctions and dogmas, has prepared men's minds for new and greater efforts. Out of the contempt for mere party politics will naturally grow a desire to throw aside small and temporary remedies—to refuse to listen any longer to those who would plaster a cut finger, or burn an old wart, and call this doctoring the body politic—

28 *The Nation,* Dublin, 1842-97.

The Nation was founded by three young barristers, Charles Gavan Duffy, John Blake Dillon and Thomas Davis, all of whom had journalistic experience. They were the central figures in the group later known as Young Ireland. *The Nation* was one of the major nationalist newspapers for over fifty years. On its first day of publication the print-run of 12,000 copies was sold out, and within a short time it had a higher circulation than any other newspaper in Ireland.

The editorial from the first issue is by Davis and sets out the philosophy of the paper, a form of pluralist and moderate nationalism. The paper also had an important cultural dimension and included poems and other literary matter. When Davis died in 1845 he was succeeded by John Mitchel; he edited the paper for two years before going on to found the more extreme *United Irishman.*

An illustration from the 1880s showing Davis, Duffy and Dillon planning *The Nation* in the Phoenix Park.

Vol. IX.—No. 41.—Whole No. 457.   NEW YORK, SATURDAY, JUNE 7, 1879.—TWELVE PAGES.   PRICE FIVE CENTS.

THE MOORE CENTENARY AT THE NEW YORK ACADEMY OF MUSIC, MAY 28.

29 *The Irish World*, New York, file 1876–1980.

The Irish World was a radical weekly newspaper which circulated in America and in Ireland. It was founded and edited by Patrick Ford (1837–1913) who was born in Galway and fought on the Union side in the American Civil War. Generally, it reflected Ford's extreme nationalist views. From its foundation in 1870, the paper supported the main nationalist movements, including the Fenians, the Land League and Home Rule. It had large sales in Ireland, and was closely monitored by the authorities who banned it on a number of occasions. The Library's holdings of the paper include files bearing the stamp of the Chief Secretary's Office Library in Dublin Castle. They were acquired after the British withdrawal in 1922.

    The issue of 7 June 1879 reported on the celebration for the centenary of the birth of the poet Thomas Moore (1779–1852) at the New York Academy of Music.

30 *The Illustrated London News,* London, 1842–1987.

The Illustrated London News was originally a weekly newspaper, but in this century it gradually changed its style and format to that of a magazine. It pioneered the use of illustration in periodical literature. On occasion, it covered Irish affairs in considerable detail, and is a major source of pictorial documentation for the Famine and the Land War. The paper also gave comprehensive coverage to international affairs, and the plate shown here, from the issue of 10 June 1871, relates to the burning of the Tuileries in Paris. This disaster occurred during the revolt by the Left following the French defeat in the war with Prussia. The Tuileries had served as a royal palace since the sixteenth century, and was last occupied by the Emperor Napoleon III and Empress Eugénie who were deposed the previous September.

77

an Claiḋeaṁ Soluir

[An Claidheamh Soluis.]
· aʒur Fáinne an lae. ·

"REGISTERED AS A NEWSPAPER."

Leaḃar V, Uiṁir 14.
Vol. V.   No. 14.

Baile Áṫa Cliaṫ, Meiṫeaṁ 13, 1903.
DUBLIN, JUNE 13, 1903.

Pinginn.
One Penny.

Cúrraí an tSaoġail

Sʒéala ó na Cúiʒ Cúiʒí.

iar-Connaċta.

Saor-Ċeárpaiḋeaċt Ġaeḋealaċ.

An lá ḋeireaḋ ḋe ṁí na Bealtaine tuʒ mé cuaird ʒo veí lár-Connaċta, nó ʒo mbeaċta mé ṫreoil ar an Spioéal. Aʒur tá an baile rin ruiḋte ar ḃárr na paláa ar ḃeiʒ na ʒráime, 7 cuan caoṁ-áluinn na Ġaillṁe ar a aʒaiḋ amaċ ó ṫear, aʒur tairnʒe fíaéaine 7 vanaċ mór porcaiʒ ar a cúl 7 ṫuaiḋ. Tá an ceanntar rin ó ḃárr ʒo loċ 'ac Oiré ʒo véir tá ṫreoil a ḃear ʒo raḃaʒe ar na háiceaeaeaiḃ ir Ġaeḋealaiʒe 'nÉirinn. Táer ar an Spioéal tá an Ġaeḋilʒe le cloirteáil ʒo boʒ ḃinn 7 aʒ uapal, aʒ reaṅ 7 aʒ óʒ. Tá rí le cloirteáil aʒ na rip ar oḃair ʒaéa ceaḃ 'ná'n bóéar. Tá rí le cloirteáil 'n álréiḃ ʒaéa Doṁnaiʒ a'n Baʒar Papaḃríʒe, an táéaur Ó Connaire. Tá rí le cloirteáil aʒ an Doctúin aʒ freaʒraḃ 7 aʒ póinʒire ar ḃaoiniḃ tinne. Tá rí le cloirteáil aʒ an Máiʒirtir-rʒoile aʒur ó́ ceaʒair aiʒe ʒo 'ċuile ḃuine ina rʒoil. Aʒur ḃíʒeaṁ 7 ropla na Ġaeḋilʒe rin le cloirteáil aʒ an Oireaċtar i mḃliaéaina aʒ ḃuine ne an Breacaiʒeáin ir fearr i nÉirinn—Comar Ó Ceilrc.

Aċt ní aʒ cṫrainreaċ na Ġaeḋilʒe rin-aṁáil ʒur ṁuir tá a ḃeinʒ naé aṅ cṫreoil tá aʒ ruaṅ iná tʒeal aʒur ċruairiʒ náḃ paéar aṅ aṁáil i ndearaṁ. ʒur ḋe ʒaile ḃeinʒ nó tá beire ḃeanaṁ na tí ó aṅ aʒ uṅ aʒ an aéuar ó Connaire, Baʒar an paḃaḃríʒe rin.

Aʒur anoir nuair atá cruoḃ aʒur ʒniroṁ nua, aʒ neapreaṁ ar na Ġaeḋilʒ ó na tíre, 7 an teanʒa Ġaeḋealaṅ ḋá cuir ar ḃun, aʒur an ceóil Ġaeḋealaṅ ḋá ḃeinṁ ar beoʒ ḃinn, aʒur ʒnara Ġaeḋealaċ aʒ teaċt 7 ʒcoṅ—ʒo cinnte neapḃéa níor ḃ'féiriʒ ḋan áir a ḃaʒáil ar peitteaṅḃuir aṅ lár-Connaṅaċ—ṫríoṅ-ḃainʒeaṅ na Ġaeḋilʒe—le cóir 7 coṁṅʒ a ḃéanaṁ ann, ar an tḃear-Ċeárpaiḋeaṅ ʒlan Ġaeḋealaṅ a teaḃair ar a ḃaiʒ, map ḃí na tíre reo ruaṁ a ḃí Ġaeḋil ar a ʒcoáir i nÉireann aʒur an ṫiṅ raoi na-a ʒcoṅaile áṅaṁṁṅ féin aca.

Tá an táp 7 coirʒ rin ná ḃéanaṁ pan áit—aʒur ḃéiʒ ḃeilb 7 ḃéanaṁ, Ġóar 7 oppe na-ḃéaʒleapʒ na tír Ġaeḋealaṅ le Cill-Caininn a pinne Ḃrian Ḋópuina i nḃinir Ċalrpa.

Droiċeaḋ Cromil.

"IISY, old dame, can you tell me where Cromwell's Bridge is?"

"Cromil's Bridge, is it? I can that thin. Go down into the lowest depths o' the blackest pits o' Hell—there you'll find Cromil an' his bridges too."

Droiċeaḋ ó Áréaḋ coʒaiḋ loir na Saranaiʒ ḃo cuir an coirʒ reo ar peanḃṁola ar Ġáar an ḃleanna Ṡaṅ ṫleanna Ṡaṅ, 7 pin ó áḃar an ṫ́neaḃṁa a ḃuair ar pocail, naeṅ.

Ir ḃpéaṅ liom a ṫ́ḃṫaíʒ naé ṫo ṁuinncir ṁóir na Ġáaro an ṫ́neaṅ-ḃean ʒḃairḃe reo. Níor puʒaḃ tá ḃaonne ner na manʒaṅoiʒṁ ʒaláiner a ċoṁnuiʒeann ar an ʒṅpon ṫreaḃpa map reo a ṁáiʒ a ḃaiʒo Ḃéaáiṁṁ an baill aʒ í, map onḃir, ir ṫ́neaṅ, ṫor na Saranaṁ. Ir ḃpéaṅ liom a ṫ́ṁuinncir Uí Ḃruin ó Ḋún Maoṁṁḃaaiʒo [...]

Feir loċ Ʒarmain.

31 *An Claidheamh Soluis,* Dublin, 1898-1938.

An Claidheamh Soluis (the sword of light) was a bilingual weekly newspaper. It was published by the Gaelic League and was intended to promote the revival of the Irish language and Irish culture generally. The contributors included a number of the architects of the 1916 Rising, most notably Eoin MacNeill, The O'Rahilly and Patrick Pearse, all of whom edited the paper for a period. Pearse became editor in March 1903. He enlarged the format from tabloid to full newspaper size; he also improved the design and introduced illustrations. The new style, however, was not commercially viable and within a year the paper reverted to a less extravagant format. The issue of 13 June 1903 reported on the Wexford Feis Ceoil, and included a round-up of news from Connacht which Pearse knew relatively well.

Patrick Pearse.

32 *The Belfast News-Letter,* Belfast, file 1757- .

The Belfast Newsletter (now the *News Letter*) was first published in 1737 and is the oldest surviving newspaper in Ireland. It was founded by Francis Joy, a Belfast printer and papermaker who was the grandfather of the United Irishman, Henry Joy McCracken. He pioneered the use of Irish paper which he produced in his own mill at Ballymena. The newspaper was one of the most successful in the country; before the end of the eighteenth century it had a circulation of two to three thousand copies per issue, which was high for the time. Over the years it has always included local, national and international news, and the file is now a major source for the social, economic and political history of the past two and a half centuries.

  The illustration shows Belfast City Hall which was opened on 1 August 1906 by the Lord Lieutenant, the Earl of Aberdeen.

THE NEW CITY HALL.

33 *Irish Independent,* Dublin, 1891- .

The *Irish Daily Independent* was established by the Parnellite wing of the Irish Parliamentary Party in 1891. In 1900 it was taken over by the Dublin businessman, William Martin Murphy, who later re-launched it as the *Irish Independent*. In the twenties it supported the Treaty and became identified with Cumann na nGaedheal and later with Fine Gael.

   The page selected to represent the paper records Ireland's accession to the EEC. Denmark, the United Kingdom and Ireland became members at midnight on 31 December 1972. The following day, 1 January 1973, most newspapers had extensive coverage. The *Irish Independent* profiled the EEC Commissioner, Dr Patrick J. Hillery, who later became President of Ireland.

81

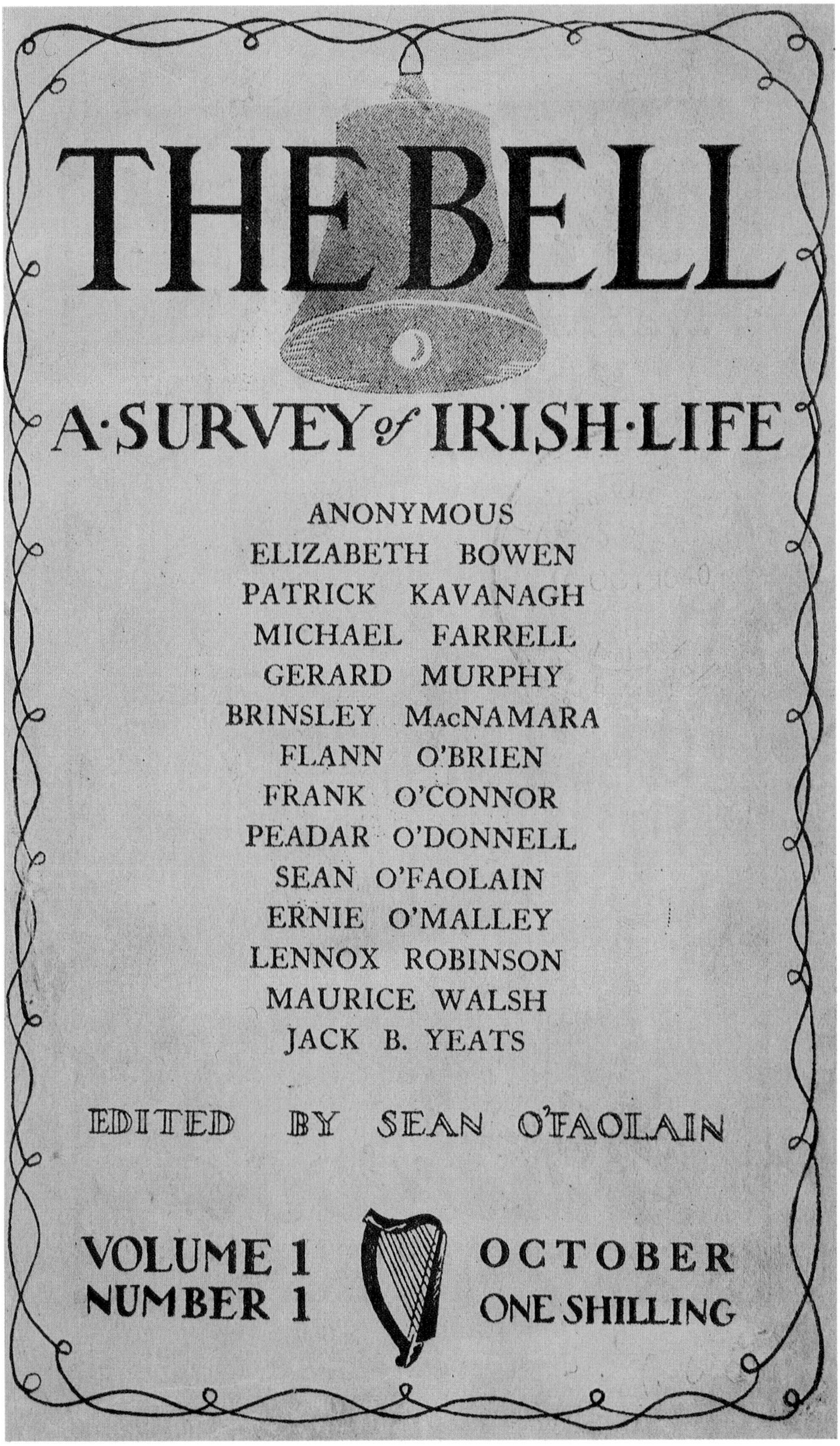

THE BELL

A·SURVEY of IRISH·LIFE

ANONYMOUS
ELIZABETH BOWEN
PATRICK KAVANAGH
MICHAEL FARRELL
GERARD MURPHY
BRINSLEY MacNAMARA
FLANN O'BRIEN
FRANK O'CONNOR
PEADAR O'DONNELL
SEAN O'FAOLAIN
ERNIE O'MALLEY
LENNOX ROBINSON
MAURICE WALSH
JACK B. YEATS

EDITED BY SEAN O'FAOLAIN

VOLUME 1
NUMBER 1

OCTOBER
ONE SHILLING

VOL. XIX, No. 11.   DECEMBER, 1954

THE BELL

EDITED BY PEADAR O'DONNELL

ASSOCIATE EDITOR ANTHONY CRONIN

CONTENTS

THE BELL is published monthly at 14 Lower O'Connell Street, Dublin. Telephone 40951. MSS. must be accompanied by a stamped addressed envelope. The yearly subscription is 26/-, post free.

34 *The Bell,* Dublin, 1940–48, 1950–54.

In addition to newspapers, the National Library has an extensive collection of periodicals which is international in range. It represents a wide range of interests and includes titles published by a large number of learned institutions in Ireland and abroad; many of the files extend back to the eighteenth century. To represent the collection we have selected the first issue of *The Bell,* a relatively short-run literary journal which was noted for its radical views and provocative style. It was edited first by Seán O'Faoláin and later by Peadar O'Donnell. In practice the pair collaborated throughout the life of *The Bell;* initially O'Donnell managed the business side and in its latter years O'Faoláin contributed many notable articles and letters, including 'The Bishop of Galway and *The Bell*'.

The contributors included some of the leading writers of the day and the magazine also provided an outlet for many new writers. As well as literary matter, it included articles on a wide range of current issues, including censorship, the Irish language and international affairs.

V. PRINTS AND DRAWINGS

As was the case with most of the National Library's collections, the collection of prints and drawings originated with the RDS Library and the Joly Library. In the case of prints and drawings, however, the Joly Library was so well endowed that, even now more than a century later, the Joly items amount to over three-quarters of the National Library's entire holdings of prints and drawings. The Joly material consists of 70,000 individual prints and several thousand albums of prints; in addition there are extensive holdings of original drawings and watercolours.

Among the more noteworthy of the Joly items are the many spectacular topographical prints and drawings depicting the cities and towns and the sights and beauty spots of Europe and the world at large. Similarly engaging are the contemporary illustrations of historical events, the plans of battles and the plates of military and naval costume. They recall a multitude of bloody wars and hard-fought campaigns in various corners of Europe back to the sixteenth century, with the Seven Years War, the Napoleonic Wars and the Crimean War being especially well documented. The Joly material is particularly valuable in that it is international in range, and includes material from most European countries. This is all the more important as over the years the National Library has generally purchased only prints and drawings of Irish interest, and without the Joly foundation the present collection would be relatively insular.

The National Library's other foundation collection, the RDS Library, had only a small number of individual prints or drawings. It did, however, include many fine folio volumes with superb engraved plates, particularly in subject areas such as natural history, architecture and topography. The RDS also made an important indirect contribution to the National Library collection, in that the schools maintained by the (Royal) Dublin Society provided training in drawing and design for many of the artists and engravers whose work is represented, for instance, John Comerford, Hugh Douglas Hamilton, George Petrie, Thomas Sautell Roberts and Martin Archer Shee.

The collection has developed considerably since the foundation of the National Library, with the main expansion taking place in the Irish sections which have been the most heavily used over the years. The Irish topographical collection is particularly extensive and important. The published *Catalogue of Irish Topographical Prints and Original Drawings* (by Rosalind M. Elmes, revised by Michael Hewson 1975) lists the Library's holdings in this area at about 6,000 items. The collection has many fine engravings and etchings, especially from the relatively affluent decades immediately preceding the Act of Union in 1800 and also from the first half of the nineteenth century. They were mostly published in London or Dublin, and were often hand coloured and issued in folio volumes or as individual prints suitable for framing. Of the artists featured, Samuel Frederick Brocas, Jonathan Fisher, James Malton, George Petrie and Thomas Sautell Roberts are among the more notable. Generally, the artists (and the publishers) favoured romantic scenery and tourist attractions such as Killarney, the Giant's Causeway and Glendalough. Of the cities and towns only Dublin, with over 500 loose prints, is well documented; the others have at best a dozen or two.

The Irish topographical drawings record the state of the landscape and the buildings thereon over more than three hundred years. The seventeenth century is represented by the pen-and-ink sketches of towns and castles by the English tourist, Thomas Dingley; and by watercolour prospects of ports and fortifications which were executed at the behest of James II by the military engineer, Thomas Phillips. Among the more important memorials of the eighteenth and nineteenth centuries are the renderings of architectural antiquities by Gabriel Beranger and by Francis and Daniel Grose, the views of country seats by John Preston Neale, and the watercolours of Killarney by Mary Herbert. Where possible, the Library acquires contemporary drawings and watercolours, and the collection features work by various twentieth-century artists, including Jack B. Yeats, Brian Coghlan and Alison Rosse.

The Irish topographical drawings are complemented by a collection of 5,000 architectural drawings, mainly of the eighteenth and nineteenth centuries. They include ground plans, elevations and sketches for public buildings, churches, houses and outbuildings; there are also designs for ceilings, mantlepieces and other features. Among those whose work is represented are Robert Adam, Thomas Cooley, James Gandon, Francis Johnston and Michael Stapleton.

There is a good collection of Irish historical illustrations, both originals and prints. They date from the seventeenth century onwards and the main concentrations coincide with the peaks of military or political activity and the turning points of Irish history. For instance, the Williamite War, the 1798 Rising and Daniel O'Connell's campaigns for Catholic Emancipation and Repeal of the Union are all well documented. Aspects of economic history, agriculture and the industrial revolution are also featured. The railway was a particularly popular subject, beginning with Andrew Nicholl's evocative aquatints of the Dublin to Kingstown line published in 1834.

The collection of portraits amounts to about 20,000 items, of which some 3,000 are Irish. The *Catalogue of Engraved Irish Portraits* (by Rosalind M. Elmes, 1938) lists the 1,100 subjects, the artists and the engravers. Some subjects are recorded in only a single portrait but others do considerably better; for instance, Dean Swift has over thirty engravings and Wellington over two hundred. Many of the finest portrait engravers are represented, among them Francesco Bartolozzi, George Vertue and Charles Turner, and the Irishmen, Henry Brocas, John Brooks, James McArdell and John Kirkwood.

The Library's holdings of prints and drawings constitute a major art collection of international significance and represent the work of some hundreds of artists and engravers, foreign as well as Irish. It is an important source for the history of art, and especially for the history of engraving and reproduction processes. It is also a productive source for study of the landscape, history, society and personalities of Ireland, Britain and continental Europe over the past four hundred years. With the present proliferation of illustrated books, magazines and television documentaries, the collection is being used increasingly by authors and their editors and by television producers and their researchers. They are all in search of the right picture to point up the written or the spoken text, hoping thereby, perhaps, to save themselves a thousand words.

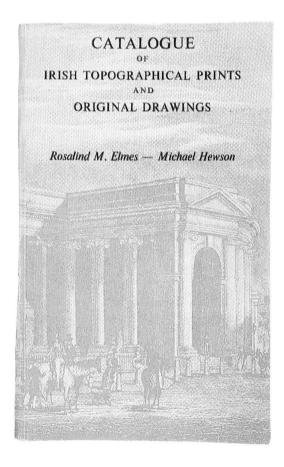

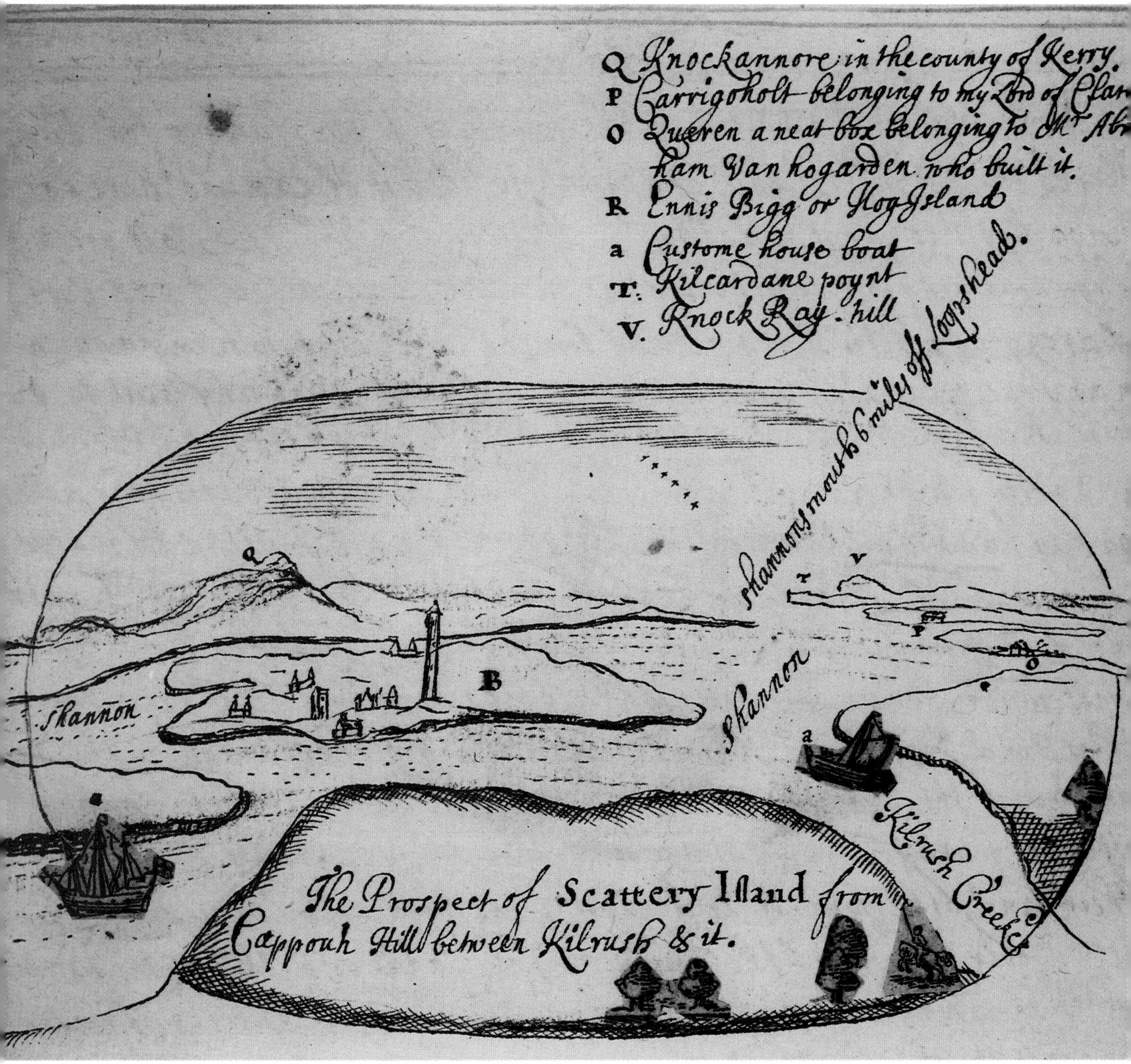

Q. Knockannore in the county of Kerry.
P. Carrigoholt belonging to my Lord of Clan...
O. Queren a neat box belonging to Mr Ab...
   ham Van hogarden who built it.
R. Ennis Bigg or Hog Island
a. Custome house boat
T. Kilcardane poynt
V. Knock Ray hill

shannons mouth 6 miles off Loopshead.

shannon

Shannon

Kilrush Creek

The Prospect of Scattery Island from
Cappouh Hill between Kilrush & it.

35 A manuscript volume by Thomas Dingley with **'Observations in a Voyage in the Kingdom of France'** and **'Observations in a Voyage through the Kingdom of Ireland'**, *c.* 1681. (Ms 392.)

Thomas Dingley (or Dineley) was an English antiquary who wrote these accounts of his travels in France (*c.* 1675) and in Ireland (1680-81). The volume is remarkable for its many pen-and-ink drawings of cities, towns, churches, castles and other features in both countries. While some of the Irish castles are copied from Stafford's *Pacata Hibernia,* most of the drawings are original and in some cases are the earliest known depictions of the subject. Among the counties represented are Dublin, Carlow, Tipperary, Limerick, Clare and Cork. Clare is particularly well covered, due possibly to the fact that Dingley's patron, the Duke of Beaufort, had connections with the O'Briens, Earls of Thomond.

Scattery Island, in the estuary of the Shannon, is best known for its association with St Senan who founded a monastery there in the sixth century. It remained an important ecclesiastical centre for several centuries and the remains of the round tower and a number of churches still survive. The castle to the left of the round tower is believed to have been built around 1577 and appears as a flat-topped turret; it is not recorded in any other illustration and only traces of it now remain. The key reads:

Q. Knockannore in the county of Kerry.

P. Carrigoholt, belonging to my Lord of Clare.

O. Queren, a neat box [lodge] belonging to Mr Abraham Vanhogarden who built it.

R. Ennis Bigg or Hog Island.

A. Customehouse boat.

T. Kilcardane Poynt.

V. Knock Ray hill.

G. Kneller ad vivum pinx: P. Vandrebanc sculp: et exc 1689.

The Reverend   and Valiant
Mr George Walker Governour of London Derry

Offered by his most humble Servant P. Vandrebanc.

90

36 Godfrey Kneller, **'The Reverend and Valiant Mr George Walker Governour of London Derry',** engraved by Peter Vandrebanc, London, 1689. (39 x 30cm.)

On 18 April 1689, James II was refused entry into Derry and the famous siege (one hundred and five days) began. The Reverend George Walker (1618-90) became joint governor and organised the successful defence of the city. After the siege was raised he was sent to London with a loyal address to King William III. He was rapturously received by the public and congratulated by William. His portrait was painted by the German-born artist Godfrey Kneller (1646-1723), who portrayed ten reigning monarchs and many of the leading personalities of the day. The portrait was engraved by the French engraver Peter Vandrebanc (Van der Banc). It was acquired by the Joly Library. George Walker was killed the following July at the Battle of the Boyne.

The Walker Monument, Derry, from a nineteenth-century engraving.

37 Thomas Phillips, **'A Prospect of Charles Fort'**, 1685. (100 x 61 cm; Ms 2557.)

Thomas Phillips was an official military engineer whom James II sent to Ireland in 1685 to survey and report on the country's fortifications. In the course of this work he produced a number of watercolour maps and prospects of towns, castles and fortifications, most of which were on the coast (see also no. 83). The Library has acquired duplicate sets of his Irish maps and prospects: one purchased from the great library at Cheltenham built up by Sir Thomas Phillipps in the nineteenth century, and the other with the Ormond Papers from Kilkenny Castle purchased in 1946.

Charles Fort, near Kinsale, Co. Cork, was built in 1677 to the design of Sir William Robinson (architect of the Royal Hospital, Kilmainham, Co. Dublin) and named in honour of Charles II. It was occupied continuously until the British withdrawal in 1922; it was destroyed by a fire during the Civil War.

Prospect of the Parliament House, in College Green DUBLIN. | Veüe de l'hôtel du Parlement rüe du Collège green de DUBLIN.

Published according to Act of Parliament

London, Printed for Robt. Sayer Map & Printseller at the Golden Buck near Serjeants Inn, Fleet Street.

38 Joseph Tudor, **'A Prospect of the Parliament House in College Green, Dublin',** London, [1753]. (22 x 37 cm; 590 TBa.)

This hand–coloured mezzotint (half-tone) engraving on paper is number five of a series of six views of Dublin by Joseph Tudor; the inscription is in English and French. It gives the view from Trinity College, with the Parliament House on the right, and College Green in the foreground leading into Dame Street in the distance. The engraving is a fairly accurate, though somewhat flamboyant representation. Tudor tended to take liberties with his subjects and here he seems to have made the vista more expansive than it was at the time; this is some years before Dame Street was improved by the Wide Streets Commission established by Parliament in 1757. A feature of the prospect is the large number of houses with the gables facing the street, a style which became common towards the end of the seventeenth century; some of the houses have the distinctive decorative Dutch gables.

   Joseph Tudor (1695?-1759) was a landscape painter who lived in Dame Street. Many of his paintings were engraved in Dublin and London. Here, the engraver is not given but it is thought that it was James McArdell, a Dubliner then working in London, who is regarded as the leading mezzotint scraper (engraver) of the period.

39 Gabriel Beranger, **'A Collection of Drawings of the Principal Antique Buildings of Ireland',** 1765-1774. (22 x 28 cm; 1958 TX.)

Gabriel Beranger (1729-1817) was a professional artist who was born in Rotterdam in Holland of a family of French Huguenots and settled in Dublin in 1750. He devoted considerable time to sketching antiquities around the country but especially around Dublin. Two small albums of his field sketches are in the Royal Irish Academy. Two large albums of his watercolours also survive, one of which is in the Academy and the other is this National Library volume which was purchased in 1937. It has ninety-

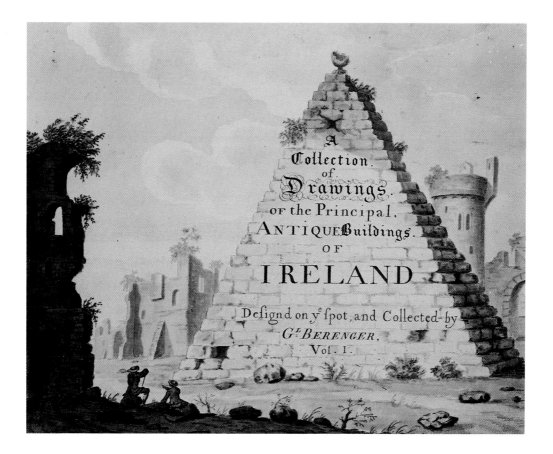

nine drawings, mostly in watercolour; about half are based on Beranger's own sketches and the rest are copies of works by other artists. Though lacking in artistic vision, Beranger was a painstaking and accurate draughtsman, and the album is an important record of many buildings which have either disappeared or fallen into ruin.

Ballyowen Castle was drawn by Beranger in 1766. It is about a mile from Lucan, off the Lucan to Clondalkin road near Esker. It probably dates from the sixteenth century but the large windows and the porch are eighteenth-century features. A succession of owners lived there in the seventeenth and eighteenth centuries, but it had fallen into ruin by the 1830s. At present all that remains is the ground storey which has vestiges of a modern roof.

40 Section of the dairy at Abbeville, Malahide, Co. Dublin, by James Gandon,
c. 1790s. (22 x 27 cm; AD1763.)

The architect, James Gandon, was born in London but moved to Dublin in 1781.
Around the 1790s he was commissioned by John Beresford (brother of the First
Marquess of Waterford) to design a dairy, stable, bridge and gate for his house,
Abbeville, which was named after the birthplace of his first wife in Northern France.
The drawing, executed in pen, wash and watercolour, is one of two sections of the
dairy in the Library's collection of architectural drawings. The Library also has a
number of other Gandon drawings, including some for Slane Castle, Emo Court,
Co. Laois, Carrigglas Manor, Co. Longford, and the Custom House and the
Four Courts in Dublin.

James Gandon (1742-1823), with the Custom House in the background; engraved
from a painting by Horace Hone.

41 'Arrestation du Roi et sa Famille Désertant du Royaume', [Paris ?, *c.* 1791].
(25 x 38 cm.)

This etching is one of a large number of historical scenes, cartoons and caricatures
relating to the French Revolution which were acquired with the Joly Library. It
depicts the arrest of Louis XVI, Marie Antoinette, their two children and the King's
sister during their attempt to flee to safety. The family slipped out of Paris undetected
on the night of 20 June 1791 and headed east towards the German border. They
travelled over one hundred miles but were eventually recognised and arrested at
Varennes. They were escorted back to Paris and the royal couple were guillotined the
following year.

The arrest of the French royal family excited great interest throughout Europe and
was represented in a variety of prints, of which many were of a satirical nature. This
anonymous example is inaccurate in a number of details but it evokes the atmosphere
of the occasion; versions of it were available outside France within a matter of weeks.
Etching is a type of engraving in which the elements of the image are burnt into the
printing plate with acid; it was commonly used for this type of ephemeral publication
as prints could be turned out quickly while the story was live. This one is hand
coloured in a loose way; the colouring is apparently contemporary and the livery and
costume colours seem to be realistic.

ARRESTATION DU ROI ET SA FAMILLE DESERTANT DU ROYAUME ..

GOLD MINES, COUNTY of WICKLOW.

In the Fore-ground are several Figures employed in working or buddling; in the Middle ground they are seen digging & barrowing the Earth, which contains the particles of Gold : on the first discovery of these Mines, pieces of pure Gold were found valued at eighty pounds and upwards, one of which may be seen at the Leverian Museum. The Scene closes with Croughan and the adjoining Hills.

42 Thomas Sautell Roberts, **'Gold Mines, County of Wicklow',** engraved by J. Bluck, London, 19 May 1804. (48 x 60 cm; 1875 TC.)

Substantial quantities of gold were mined in Co. Wicklow in the prehistoric period, and surface deposits have since been found from time to time along the streams flowing off Croghan Mountain in the south of the county. Small amounts were extracted in the period 1795-98 and the operation is recorded in this aquatint. The inscription describes the process:

> 'In the foreground are several figures employed in working or buddeling [washing]; in the middle ground they are seen digging & barrowing the earth, which contains the particles of gold: on the first discovery of these mines, pieces of pure gold were valued at eighty pounds and upwards, one of which may be seen at the Levarian Museum. The scene closes with Croughan and the adjoining hills'.

The Levarian [Leverian] Museum was established in London in the late eighteenth century by Sir Ashton Lever; it was sold and dispersed in 1806.

Thomas Sautell Roberts (*c*.1760–1826) was born in Waterford and studied at the Dublin Society Drawing Schools. He worked in London for a period but was back in Dublin at the time this work was published. He specialised in topography and architecture, and many of his paintings were engraved in aquatint; this was a type of etching which gave fine gradations of tone in the manner of a watercolour – hence the term aquatint. The Library has over thirty of Robert's engraved works. This specimen has been coloured by hand.

43 A view of Wexford by Captain H. Mitchell (96th Regiment), 20 May 1820;
engraved by Short and Sutherland, London. (70 x 128 cm; 1796 TD.)

This engraving offers the only known full-scale depiction of Wexford in the
pre-famine period. The perspective is taken from the Castlebridge side of the River
Slaney. It focuses particular attention on the wooden bridge, notorious as the scene of
a much-publicised massacre of prisoners which was precipitated by the collapse of
United Irish discipline in the last chaotic hours of the 'Republic of Wexford'. The
bridge itself had been constructed in the mid-1790s by Lemuel Cox, the celebrated
American engineer, and the drawing is carefully detailed, even down to the toll gate
on its eastern entry.

Wexford had a population of *c.* 10,000 in 1820, and was a relatively vibrant market
town, specialising in malting barley for the Dublin distilling industry; the sailing
vessels to the left of the bridge were used mainly for carrying malt to Dublin. Already
though, concern was being expressed about silting which was slowly choking the
commercial harbour to death. The town itself is shown in profile, and still retaining
its medieval shape and character. The Vikings had settled here on an old ferry site,
and gave the town its peculiarly appropriate name *Weiss-fiord* (the harbour of the
mud-flats). Later, the Normans extended the town and walls; its linear shape,
its crowded, crooked streets, and its dense building fabric are well captured in
the engraving.

This View of the CITY OF WEXFORD, &c with Perspective Dedicated to Field Marshal H.R.H. the DUKE OF YORK.
By His Royal Highness most Devoted Servant

44 Derrynane Abbey, Waterville, Co. Kerry, by John Fogarty, engraved by
R. Havell, London, [1833]. (42 x 57 cm; 1063 TC.)

This aquatint with hand-colouring shows the ancestral home of Daniel O'Connell.
He inherited the house in 1825 from his uncle, Maurice ('Hunting Cap') O'Connell.
The house dated in part from the early eighteenth century and took its name from
the ruined abbey which appears in the background. The Liberator is depicted hat-in-
hand in the foreground. The hurling scene on the left is one of the few depictions of
the sport in the early nineteenth century. The flag on the house was presumably put
in by the artist to acknowledge O'Connell's achievement in securing Catholic
Emancipation two years previously. It features the gold harp which was regarded as a
national symbol since the Middle Ages and now appears on the presidential flag. The
print is based on a watercolour made in 1831; it has the date and the name of the
artist in manuscript.

Cloictheach. Cloyne, Co Cork.

W.F.Wakeman
1892.

45 William Frederick Wakeman, **'Cloigh Thighe or Round Towers of Ancient Ireland'**, *c.* 1890-95. (page 34 x 24 cm; 2007 TX.)

W. F. Wakeman (1822-1900) worked for a period as a draughter and assistant with the Ordnance Survey. Later he taught art at Portora Royal School and the Model School in Enniskillen. He published a number of archaeology and travel books and he contributed drawings to many of the publications of the period. This album has fifty-seven pen, ink and watercolour drawings. It was purchased in 1989 along with a companion volume of high crosses. They were both commissioned by Francis Joseph Bigger, the Belfast antiquarian.

Cloyne, Co. Cork, was the site of the monastery of St Colmán mac Lénéni who died in 606 A.D. The monastery was plundered by the Vikings a number of times in the ninth century and the one-hundred-foot tower dates from that period. Its conical roof was destroyed by lightning in 1748-9; when restored, the height was reduced and battlements were added.

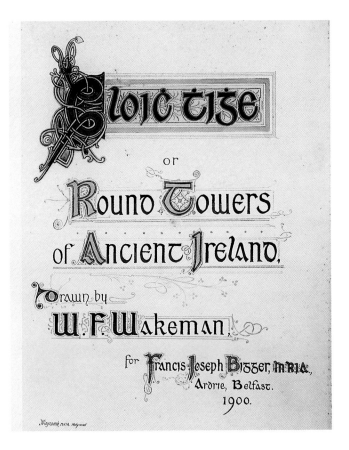

A photograph taken in 1907.

46 John Butler Yeats, a self-portrait, 1907. (38 x 28 cm.)

John Butler Yeats (1839-1922) was born at Tullylish, Co. Down, where his father, the Rev. William Butler Yeats, was the Church of Ireland rector. In 1863 he married Susan Pollexfen of Sligo. They had four children, all of whom had remarkable literary or artistic talent: William Butler, Susan Mary, Elizabeth Corbet and Jack Butler. He qualified as a barrister but did not practice and instead went to London to train as an artist. He specialised in portraiture and was elected RHA in 1892. In 1908 he moved to New York where he spent the remainder of his life.

The self-portrait is watercolour on card. It was acquired with a collection of his drawings donated by his daughters in 1924; the collection includes portraits of members of the family and of various literary and political personalities of the time.

VI. PHOTOGRAPHS

The collection of photographs amounts to approximately 250,000 items, of which the vast majority are of Irish interest. While most have been acquired in this century, a very large percentage date from the last century, mainly from 1850 onwards. Many of the photographs are prints which have been received as individual items or as groups mounted in albums. The majority, however, are in the form of negatives, either glass plate or sheet film, and have been acquired mainly from professional photographic firms. The photographs were generally acquired for the purpose of documenting Ireland and its people, and the collection mainly records important events, social life, architecture and topography. However, while factors such as aesthetics or production techniques were not of primary concern, the collection includes work by many distinguished photographers and it illustrates the main advances in photography.

Experiments were carried out by various people over many years, but it was only in the early nineteenth century that viable photographs were first produced. Two distinct processes were made public in 1839, that of Louis Daguerre in France and William Henry Fox Talbot in England. The Daguerre process produced an image on a metal plate; while the images were of high quality, the process had the disadvantage that it was once-off, and additional copies could not be made without repeating the whole operation. It did, however, bring portraiture within the reach of the ordinary person, and soon there were studios in Dublin and other cities providing the service. As it was not possible to produce multiple copies of daguerreotypes, those of public figures were often published as engravings or lithographs. The Library has a number of daguerreotypes and some engravings and lithographs of personalities such as Daniel O'Connell and the Duke of Wellington.

The Fox Talbot process involved a paper negative from which multiple positive prints (calotypes) could be run off on salt paper. This was the more practical process; while daguerreotype photography is still used for some specialist purposes, variations of the Fox Talbot negative-positive process have predominated since about 1850. But, for a number of years the process was generally used only by the gentry or aristocracy as it was governed by patent, and Fox Talbot tended to issue licences only to people of his own class. Among the Irish people favoured with a licence were Edward King Tenison and his wife Louisa of Kilronan Castle, Co. Roscommon. Albums of their work dating from *c.*1850 are among the Library's earliest holdings.

A major advance took place in 1851 with the discovery of the wet-plate (collodion) process by Frederick Scott Archer; this involved painting the plates with emulsion immediately before use. It was possible to take photographs out of doors by using a portable darkroom, and wet plates were widely used for producing views of scenic spots for sale to tourists. The Library has acquired several thousand wet-plate glass negatives, including the Stereoscopic Collection, which consists of 3,000 negatives from the period 1860-80. These produced twin images which gave a three-dimensional effect when viewed together in a stereoscope. At the time, published stereo photographs were extremely popular and some photographers specialised in catering for the demand.

Wet-plate negatives became obsolete in the early 1880s and were superseded by dry plates which did not have to be prepared on the spot, and photography out of doors became a relatively simple operation. Most of the Library's collections of glass plates from the 1880s to the 1950s are dry plate, and include the Lawrence, Eason, Valentine, Poole and Wynne collections. These were all generated by commercial studios, the first three of which specialised in topographical views from around the country which they sold as prints or published as postcards. Poole and Wynne, the former in Waterford and the latter in Castlebar, concentrated mainly on portraiture.

The Library has a good collection of photographs taken by amateurs, mainly members of the landed gentry. Most of them are in albums acquired with collections of estate papers. An early album is that of Mary, Countess of Drogheda, which has the Library's earliest holiday photographs, taken in Iceland and the Faroe Islands in 1860-62. The largest collection of this nature is the Clonbrock Collection, generated by various members of the Dillon family of Ahascragh, Co. Galway in the period 1860-1930. The Clonbrock and other gentry collections are mainly devoted to views of members of the family and their friends and relatives, particularly on festive and sporting occasions.

Many aspects of late nineteenth- and early twentieth-century Ireland are well documented in the collections. For instance, scenic spots, seaside resorts, notable buildings and the streets of cities and towns are represented in Lawrence, Eason and Valentine. The main collections rarely portray the poorer classes except incidentally or in a staged and romanticised setting. However, the Library has acquired some small collections, for instance, photographs commissioned by the Mansion House Relief Committee and the Congested Districts Board which illustrate distress and people living in bad conditions in the West around the turn of the century. Also, there are various small groups of 'snaps' taken by amateurs with 'Box-Brownies'; some of these are extremely important in that they capture people or events which are not otherwise recorded.

Political, social and cultural affairs are generally well covered. For instance, there is the Keogh Collection, generated by a Dublin firm, relating to the 1916 Rising; the Richard Mulcahy photographs which document political affairs since the foundation of the state; the Hannah Sheehy-Skeffington portfolios relating to the suffragette and feminist movements; and a large

108

number of photographs from the early days of the Abbey Theatre. In so far as possible, the Library continues to develop its holdings; among recent acquisitions are 3,000 aerial photographs taken by Captain A. C. Morgan in the fifties; over 300 Belfast scenes by Brian Hughes; 500 Dublin scenes specially commissioned from Alan O'Connor; a fine collection brought together by Pádraig Tyers depicting life on the Dingle peninsula in Co. Kerry; and the collection illustrating the history of photography in Ireland accumulated by Eddie Chandler. Finally, the Library's own photographers have built up an archive of negatives of illustrations and other items in the collections over the years; it amounts to about 15,000 negatives and is now a major photographic resource in its own right.

A wet-plate photographer at work. (G. Tissandier, *History of Photography,* London, 1876.)

110

47 William Henry Fox Talbot, *The Pencil of Nature,* London, 1844-46.

William Henry Fox Talbot (1800-1877) of Lacock Abbey, Wiltshire made his discovery in 1834, but it was not until January 1839 (some weeks after Daguerre) that he made it public. Between 1844 and 1846 he published *The Pencil of Nature,* a series of six fascicles illustrating how the process worked. It includes sample photographs in the form of salt–paper prints. The National Library holds a copy of the second of these rare fascicles with twelve of the photographs. It was originally acquired by the RDS Library. The 'ladder' photograph has been interpreted as a representation of man's ascent towards light. The attractive composition is modelled on patterns in Christian art.

PLATE XIV.

THE LADDER.

PORTRAITS of living persons and groups of figures form one of the most attractive subjects of photography, and I hope to present some of them to the Reader in the progress of the present work.

When the sun shines, small portraits can be obtained by my process in one or two seconds, but large portraits require a somewhat longer time. When the weather is dark and cloudy, a corresponding allowance is necessary, and a greater demand is made upon the patience of the sitter. Groups of figures take no longer time to obtain than single figures would

112

48 A daguerreotype taken in the United States about 1860. (One-sixth plate, case 9.5 x 8.5 cm.)

Daguerreotype photography was extremely popular in the United States and continued to thrive there much longer than was the case in Ireland. Moreover, the quality achieved was usually very good and this is a fine specimen with hand-tinting. As it has turned up in Ireland, the subject is probably Irish, possibly an emigrant who sent it home to show that he was doing well. It is mounted in an American form of case, known as a union case, which was made from thermoplastic; this example is lined with red fabric. The case was made by Holmes, Booth & Hayden, a Cincinnati firm which distributed throughout the United States. The cover has a design, 'The Highland Hunter', based on an engraving by the Irish-born artist, Francis Humphreys, which was published in 1857; Humphreys worked in Cincinnati for a period. The item was acquired in 1994.

49 The Stereoscopic Collection: 3,000 negatives, *c*.1860–1883.

Stereoscopic photographs are taken with a special camera which has two lenses and takes two near-identical photographs on the one negative. When the photographs are printed and viewed side by side in a stereoscope they blend into a single image which seems three-dimensional. William Henry Fox Talbot demonstrated the effect in 1846, but it was only when Queen Victoria showed enthusiasm for the novelty at the Great Exhibition of 1851 that it became popular.

The collection in the National Library was acquired in 1943 as part of the Lawrence Collection; it includes negatives generated by various Dublin

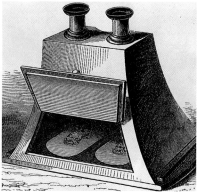

photographers, of whom the best known were
James Simonton and Frederick Holland Mares.
Lawrence acquired some of their negatives and
produced multiple prints from them for sale in his shop.

The example reproduced is of Rostrevor, County Down (S.P.1262). The
Stereoscopic Collection includes eighteen views of Rostrevor which was then a
popular seaside resort.

50 The Clonbrock Collection: 3,000 negatives and prints, *c.* 1860–1930.

The Dillons (Barons Clonbrock) were a landed family with an estate at Clonbrock near Ahascragh, Co. Galway. Various members of the family were enthusiastic amateur photographers, most notably Luke Gerald Dillon, Fourth Lord Clonbrock, and his wife Augusta (née Crofton, of Moate Park, Co. Roscommon). The couple built a studio and darkroom in the grounds of Clonbrock House.

The Clonbrock Collection was acquired when the house was sold in 1976. It documents the life of the family and includes photographs of the house and household – upstairs and downstairs – and various aspects of daily life and work on the estate. The album from which the page is reproduced includes photographs by Augusta and Luke Gerald, shown here with his wet-plate camera.

Clonbrock about 1860; it has recently been destroyed by fire.

116

Hon.ble L. G. Dillon

Hon.ble R. & L. Dillon

A. Congreve

Hon.ble Col. Spencer

Hon.ble Mary French

Westmeath Ribbonmen

John Seery

Patrick Dunne

Thomas Daly

51 Album of Fenian photographs assembled by Samuel Lee Anderson,
c. 1865-71. (Ms 5957.)

Samuel Lee Anderson was involved in intelligence work in Dublin Castle for periods before and after the Fenian Rising of 1867. His album is inscribed, 'Members of the Fenian Brotherhood, especially those who distinguished themselves by being convicted of treason-felony at the Special Commission 1865-66, or arrested under the Habeas Corpus Suspension Act, 1866'. Most of the photographs in the album were taken in prison and a number of them also appear in a manuscript in the National Archives, 'Irish Crime Records 1866-72: Description of Fenian Suspects'.

Ribbon societies were secret organisations which were active in various parts of the country from about the 1820s. They were concerned with agrarian and political issues and many members joined the Fenians, including possibly the three 'Westmeath Ribbonmen'. In 1870-71 there was an outbreak of disturbances in Co. Westmeath which provoked the Protection of Life and Property Act of June 1871, commonly known as the 'Westmeath Act'. The three were detained under its provisions and lodged in Kilmainham Jail where the photographs were taken.

Fenian prisoners exercising in an enclosure at Mountjoy Jail. *(Le Monde Illustré.)*

52 The Coolgreany Album, 1887.

This album consists of photographs taken at the notorious evictions that took place on the Brooke estate at Coolgreany, near Gorey, Co. Wexford in 1887 during the Plan of Campaign. Under the Plan, tenants on certain estates withheld their rents and lodged them in funds held by local trustees pending settlement with the landlords. The Coolgreany evictions were intensively covered in contemporary newspapers; they were also extensively photographed.

The identity of the photographer of this album is not known but it must have been a professional. It was assembled by T. Mallagy and presented to Father Laurence Farrelly, an active participant in the Plan of Campaign in Wexford. In 1992 the album was donated to the National Library by a grand-niece of Father Farrelly, Mrs Bridie Hogan of Taringa, Australia. The photograph shows one of the evicted families, the Kavanaghs from Croghan who were evicted on 8 July; they are John Kavanagh, his 87-year-old father Michael, his mother and his two children.

53 The John Joly Colour Slides: 300 items, *c.* 1890-1900.

John Joly (1857-1933) was a relative of Jasper Robert Joly who played a crucial role in the founding of the National Library. He was Professor of Geology at Trinity College, Dublin, and in the 1890s he experimented with colour photography. His system involved taking a photograph through a screen with fine red, green and blue lines onto a monochrome negative. A positive print was then made on a glass plate which was bound up with a similar screen; when projected it provided a colour image of reasonable quality. The method was rendered obsolete by the discovery of the Autochrome process in Paris some time later. The slides held by the National Library are mainly of botanical subjects.

54 The Lawrence Collection: 40,000 glass–plate negatives, *c*. 1870–1914.

The Lawrence Collection was generated by the Dublin firm of William Mervyn Lawrence (1840-1932) which was located opposite the General Post Office in Sackville Street (O'Connell Street). The firm did a good trade in portraiture, and also marketed photographs of cities, towns and tourist attractions as framed or unframed prints or as postcards. It employed a large staff including a number of photographers, most notable of whom was Robert French (1841-1917) who took most of the outdoor photographs. The portrait negatives were destroyed during the 1916 Rising; fortunately, the negatives of the views were stored separately in Rathmines and survived. They were purchased when the firm closed down in 1943.

The view shown here (R.3396) is of High Street, Enniskillen, Co. Fermanagh at the turn of the century. It is almost certainly by Robert French.

55 The Lawrence Project: 1,000 colour negatives, 1990-1991.

In 1990-91 the Federation of Local History Societies, the Federation for Ulster Local Studies, Fuji (Ireland) Limited, and the National Library co-operated in the imaginative project of re-photographing 1,000 Lawrence scenes. The purpose of the project was to provide modern graphic records of the landscapes and townscapes which had been documented by Lawrence's a hundred years before and to illustrate the subsequent changes. The modern photograph (5A 205) was taken by Walter N. Brady.

56 The Poole Collection: 60,000 glass–plate negatives, 1884–1954.

The collection was generated by the family photographic firm of A. H. Poole of
34 The Mall, Waterford. It includes a large number of studio portraits and a smaller
number of group photographs commissioned by schools, religious orders and business
concerns, taken *in situ*. The firm also acted as press photographers and the collection
includes many items documenting historic occasions and depicting social life around
the south-eastern region. The collection was acquired soon after the firm closed

In addition to the business at 34 The Mall, Poole's had this premises at 134 The Quay, next door to Reginald's Tower.

down in 1954. The order books were also acquired and provide some limited information on most of the items.

Photographs of the travelling community in Ireland have, until recently, been rare and the Library possesses only a few. This example, showing two travelling women washing clothes at an encampment near Waterford, is probably from the 1930s and is a valuable record of their distinctive life-style.

Capt. A. C. Morgan DFC.

57 The Morgan Collection: 3,000 negatives of
aerial photographs, 1954-57.

The collection was generated by Captain
Alexander Campbell Morgan, who traded as
Aerophotos. Many of the photographs were
commissioned by clients such as newspapers,
industrial concerns, builders, schools and religious
congregations. Most of the thirty-two counties are
represented. Capt. Morgan was killed at the age of
thirty-eight when his plane crashed near Shannon
Airport in January 1958. The collection was
acquired in 1991.

Portsalon, shown here, is a small holiday resort
and fishing harbour at the mouth of Lough Swilly
in Co. Donegal. The view includes the golf-
course, woods, pier, and Portsalon Hotel which
was built in the nineteenth century and has
recently been destroyed by fire.

58 Cáit (Bab) Feirtéar, by Mona Faloughi, 1992.

This portrait is one of a series taken by the Lebanese photographer, Mona Faloughi, in the Dingle area in Co. Kerry in 1992. The subject was born in Dún Chaoin (Dunquin), and is one of the greatest traditional storytellers in Ireland today. Her repertoire includes international folk-tales, legends, children's tales, proverbs, poems and *seanchas*. She learned her stories from various people in the Dún Chaoin area, but has been particularly influenced by her grandmother, Cáit Uí Shé, and her grand-aunt, Máire Ruiséal (Máire an Tobair), both of whom were also well-known storytellers. Much material has been recorded from Bab Feirtéar by the Department of Irish Folklore at University College Dublin, and by other universities. She is a frequent broadcaster on Raidió na Gaeltachta.

A traditional storyteller at the 1903 Oireachtas. (*An Claidheamh Soluis*, 13 June 1903.)

VII. MANUSCRIPTS

On its foundation, the National Library had only about a hundred manuscripts which it acquired with the RDS Library and the Joly Library, but the collection is now very extensive. It amounts to 65,000 catalogued manuscripts, comprising 750,000 individual items, and there is also a special collection of 28,000 deeds. There are 1,200 Gaelic manuscripts which are of considerable importance and are treated in Chapter VIII. In addition, there are a number of collections of estate papers which have not yet been fully processed. The collection consists almost entirely of material of Irish interest. The manuscripts vary considerably in format; many are in the form of bound volumes, but the majority consist of loose papers filed in folders and stored in boxes.

The large holdings of records from former landed estates are of particular interest for the social and economic historian. They generally include maps, leases, rentals, financial accounts and correspondence; this documentation often provides detailed information concerning relations between landlords and their tenant farmers. Most of the Library's collections of estate papers, amounting to over three hundred, were acquired as a result of a survey of estate records carried out by the Irish Manuscripts Commission between 1940 and 1980. The two surveyors, Dr Edward MacLysaght and Sir John Ainsworth, used their influence in securing many of the collections for the National Library. Among the more notable are Ormond, Lismore, Inchiquin, Clonbrock, Coolattin, Fingal, and Monteagle, most of which date from the seventeenth century onwards. Ormond also includes a collection of deeds extending back to the arrival of the Normans in the twelfth century; these are a major source for the medieval history of counties Kilkenny and Tipperary, especially with regard to land and property.

The involvement of landed proprietors in politics and civil administration at national and local levels is generally reflected in their papers. On a more personal level, the social, economic and domestic life of the families is also mirrored in records such as workmen's accounts, invoices, recipe books, cellar inventories, diaries and correspondence. For example, the lifestyle of the FitzGeralds, Dukes of Leinster, is illustrated in a series of thirty volumes of correspondence dating from the period 1750-1806, shortly before the family sold Leinster House to the Dublin Society. They include letters from a scion of the house, the celebrated patriot, Lord Edward, at a time when he was serving with the British forces in the American War of Independence.

From the other end of the political spectrum, the National Library has extensive collections of manuscripts representing most of the nationalist movements, especially from the late eighteenth century onwards. They include papers of such prominent personalities as Daniel O'Connell, architect of

Catholic Emancipation; the Young Irelander, William Smith O'Brien; and the radical agrarian reformer, James Fintan Lalor. The Land War and Home Rule periods are represented by the papers of such figures as T. C. Harrington, J. F. X. O'Brien, William O'Brien and John Redmond. As might be expected, the period 1916-23 is particularly well documented. Papers of many of the leading protagonists have been acquired, including those of Sir Roger Casement, Erskine Childers, Bulmer Hobson, Thomas MacDonagh, Eoin MacNeill, Seán T. O'Kelly, and Patrick Pearse.

With the growth of interest in economic history, one of the many facets of the Library's manuscript collection which is attracting increasing attention is its corpus of business records. The Library has acquired a number of substantial archives in this field, including records of the Prior-Wandesforde Collieries in Co. Kilkenny which date from the seventeenth century, and those of the esteemed Locke's Distillery of Kilbeggan, Co. Westmeath. An archive generated by an organisation of a very different nature is that represented by the 377 folio volumes of 'Kilmainham Papers'. These records of the Commanders-in-Chief of the Forces in Ireland from 1780 to 1890 provide detailed information on such matters as recruitment, personnel, encampments and movements of troops. Records of a central military command extending over so long a period are very rare.

Research patterns change with the times and over the past half century there is increasing emphasis on literary scholarship, and there is a parallel interest in the working papers of Irish writers. The Library now has a considerable corpus of nineteenth- and twentieth-century literary material of this nature in the form of correspondence, diaries, notes, drafts and fair copies of published and unpublished work. Among the writers whose papers are represented in the collections are Richard Brinsley Sheridan, Maria Edgeworth, Canon Sheehan, George Moore, George Bernard Shaw, Sean O'Casey, Patrick Kavanagh and Brendan Behan. Of particular importance are the large collection of papers of W. B. Yeats which was donated by his family, and the James Joyce/Paul Léon Papers which were presented in the early forties and opened to the public in 1992.

Besides actual manuscripts, the Library has extensive collections of microfilm copies of material of Irish interest overseas. Various scholars based abroad contributed to the work of locating Irish manuscripts, and the eminent palaeographer, Dr. Ludwig Bieler, was commissioned to survey early medieval material in European libraries and archives. Manuscript records in Ireland were also surveyed and filmed; they include nineteenth-century Catholic parish registers, the microfilm copies of which are a major source for genealogical research.

As a result of the Library's increasing involvement in locating, surveying and acquiring manuscripts, the Department of Manuscripts was established in 1949. Among its major achievements has been the 11-volume union catalogue listing manuscripts in the National Library and at other locations: *Manuscript Sources for the History of Irish Civilisation,* edited by the Director, R. J. Hayes, and published in 1965 by G. K. Hall of Boston. A three-volume supplement, edited by Dónall Ó Luanaigh, was published in 1979. Today, the Department of Manuscripts is located in the former premises of the Kildare Street Club at 2-3 Kildare Street – an elegant building with an attractive and spacious reading room.

A scribe as represented in Giraldus Cambrensis, *Topographia Hiberniae* (see no. 61).

SCORUM MARTYRU

SCERTAMINA QUOTIENS AD MEMORIAM
nam redeunt · totiens interim ardore
conpunctionis tangunt; Quo fit ut
fraternae caritati multum uideatur impen
dere · qui martyrum hystorias stilo stu
det memoriae commendare · Et quā
uis culpis retardantibus iter rectitudi
nis assequi ñ ualeat · incedentibus tamen
in patriam ueritatis tramitem monstrat;
Alioquin miserrimum est · feliciter nau
gantibus simui deat portum salutis · qui
patitur damna periculosae nauigationis·
Idcirco beatissimi martyris kyliani ac
sociorum eius gesta · p̄ ut possimus li
terariu notis assignare curamus · ut frat
na studia ad amorē boni operis incitem;
quia enim fialam fribus dare non pos
sumus · saltem ciatum p̄pinemus; Bea

tus kylianus scotorum genere · nobi
libus ortus parentibus · diuinę tamen

1.

A late-medieval representation of St Kilian.

59 'Sanctorum Burchardi et Kiliani Vitae', early eleventh century. (Ms 19,735; formerly Phillipps.)

This vellum manuscript in Latin is the earliest in the Library's collection, but it was purchased as recently as 1975. It includes the so-called First Life of St Burchard and the so-called Second Life of St Kilian. Both were composed before 900 A.D., by unknown authors, almost certainly at Würzburg; this copy in Carolingian script was probably made there. Kilian was an Irish missionary, popularly believed to have been born in Mullagh, Co. Cavan, but his origins are obscure. He converted Thuringia and Eastern Franconia in central Germany, and was martyred with his companions near Würzburg in 689 A.D. His cult was fostered by Burchard, an Englishman who became the first Bishop of Würzburg. Remains uncovered in 752 A.D. were locally accepted as those of the martyrs, and Bishop Burchard had the relics enshrined in his new cathedral. The cult of St Kilian was later taken up by Charlemagne and has flourished in Germany ever since.

Vniuersis sce mrls ecclie filiis. Archiepis. epis. Abbib; pbris. Regib;. Ducib;. comitib; 7oib' tam laicis qm clericis in x
fidelib'. Diarmen' nuu di rex lagnensium salt; 7 pacis spm. Notu faciu psentib; 7 posteris. qp nos tram qm diarmait uarrau
dux uanronac. p ura licenciam. in remissione peccatou suou felici abbi de ossarge 7oi eidem loci couentui. ad monasteriu
in honore beatissime di genitricis semp q; uirginis marie. scig'. t dicti abbis t didic costruendu. 7 firmam' manu tenem. 7 uri
sigilli cofirmatione munim' hee g'. tra. monachis iure pertuo t dita. dun mni. ceall mochomoc. muleann moram. ard sem -
dilli. bale ochtanugain. Raith mphoboil. Breslach. ceall nisi. Bale meic marcaig. Druim ro. Bale meic laurada. Bale
ogaillni. Bale omaille. leas meic melletira. cu omnib; suis ptinensiis. in aquis. in pascuis. in siluis. Ham ceall lainne
cum ommib' ad buc suis ptinentiis. set raith membram. 7 ard petim. tam in fluminib' qm in ptis 7 nemorib'. Donat'
uenerabilis lethglennensis epc. ad dngniam faciendam. sic meli' de notb' huic spectalit cum ura licencia. psans
monachis. qbus de sua parrochia in sui psentia pdicta terra set uru inni 7c. sure data t didit. In tialcimus
g' ne aliqs hominu de p trans cris ausu temerario. ab eisdem monachis reouum in pertuu successorib'. nec passu
pedum auterre. nec uiolentiam monastio ... ut eius gngiis si huic inferre. aut ignem apponere. siue aliqd
ab eis turtim abstrahere presumat: sed omnia in pace ecclesie integra 7 illibata dimittere. Quia siquis contra
nos inde ecctiam manum forefaciendo audacter porrexerit. res suass; habuerit. uiram si non. irreuocabiliter pdet.
Dat apud belachgautain. Teste laurentio dublinensi archiepiscopo. Donato lethglennensi episcopo.
felice abbate de ossarge. Murchad filio murchada. Murherdach filio eius. Domnallo caunanach.
Diarmait uarriain. padin. uab eda. Murchad uabrain. Dalbach eiusdem filio. 7 donncuan ua -
diarmada. 7 amleib mac coraltain;

60 Confirmation by Diarmait Mac Murchada (Dermot MacMurrough), King of Leinster, of a grant of lands; period 1162-65. (Deed 1.)

This vellum deed is the earliest in the collection; it is particularly remarkable in that it is pre-Norman. It was acquired with the Ormond Papers from Kilkenny Castle in 1946. The text is in Latin. It confirms a grant of lands made by Diarmait's liegeman Diarmait Ua Riáin (Ryan), King of Idrone (mainly in Co. Carlow), to the Cistercian foundation, Jerpoint Abbey (Co. Kilkenny). The lands were intended to endow a daughter house in the territory of Ua Riáin at Killenny, on the Kilkenny side of the Barrow near Goresbridge.

The turbulent Mac Murchada (1110-71), who is best known for his role in bringing the Normans to Ireland, had mixed relations with the church. He was honoured by St Bernard of Clairvaux, and was instrumental in founding at least three abbeys. On the other hand, he practised polygamy and was involved in such scandals as the rape of the abbess of Kildare and the abduction of Derbforgaill, consort of Tigernán Ua Ruairc, King of Breffni. Among the witnesses to the confirmation were Diarmait's brother, his illegitimate son, and his cousin, Lorcán Ó Tuathail (St Laurence O'Toole), Archbishop of Dublin. No remains of the abbey of Killenny can now be traced.

Diarmait Mac Murchada, from Giraldus Cambrensis, *Expugnatio Hibernica* (see no. 61).

137

61 Giraldus Cambrensis, ***Topographia Hiberniae*** and ***Expugnatio Hibernica,***
c. 1200. (page 28 x 17 cm; Ms 700; formerly Phillipps.)

Giraldus de Barri, better known as Giraldus Cambrensis (of Wales) was a priest who
made two visits to Ireland soon after the Norman invasion. He wrote two books in
Latin, entitled in translation, 'The Topography of Ireland' and 'The Conquest of
Ireland', both of which were completed by 1189. The works were largely
propagandist and were intended to justify the conquest by portraying the Irish as
primitive and degenerate. The page reproduced is from the *Topographia*. The two
men in a boat represent a story which Giraldus claims was relayed to him from west
of the Shannon: a traveller came across the two men who said they had never
heard of Christ or Christianity and had no knowledge of the system of weeks,
months and years.

   The manuscript is a vellum volume with transcripts of both works and was
executed around the year 1200. It also has a map of Europe (reproduced here as
no. 77) and a number of marginal illustrations; that reproduced is of the Norman
leader, Hugh de Lacy. The volume was purchased in 1945.

138

mitate qm̄ mari tr̄quillitate ap-
puuit nõ pcul faciei terre cuida̅
eis hacte̅n̄ p̄rsus ignote. de q̄m nõ
longe p̄ z cimbulam m̄ modica̅
ad se uiderunt remigantem arta̅ z
oblonga̅. in uinea̅ quide̅ z coriis animaliu̅ extra co̅gerta̅
z osuta. erant aut̅e in ea homines duo nudi om̄ino corporibꝰ
preter zonas latas de crutis anima-
lium coriis quibꝰ stringebant ha-
bebant z hybmco more comas
plongas z flauas trs humeros de-
orsum corp̄ et magna p̄te regen-
tes. De quibꝰ cu̅ audissent cp̄ de
ẜeda̅ Connaciae p̄te fuissent et
hybernica lingua loquerent̅ ur
nauem eos adduxerunt. ẜp̄i ũo
cuncta ibi q̄ uidebant tanq̄m
noua admirari ceperunt. Nauem
n̄ magnam ligneam humano
z cultu situ asserebant. q̄ nũq̄m
antea uidiant. Cum ũo panem z
caseum eis ad comedendu̅ opti-
lissent utcunq̄ ignorantes. ab-
nuerunt. Carnibꝰ trn̄ z piscibꝰ
tacte se uesti solere dicebant. et
uestibꝰ ullis utebantur n̄ coriis a-
nimaliu̅. in magna necessitate.
Et cu̅ a nautis experent an ibi ad
prandendum carnes haberent. z
responsum acciperent q̄ ẜoragesima
carnes comedi n̄ licere. ipi de q̄
drągesima nich̄ sciebant. Nec z de
anno ut̅ menses ut̅ ebdomada
quiesc̄m̄: Qui z nouinibꝰ dies

septimane censerentur. penit̅ ig-
norabant. Cum cp̄ ab ipis q̄ere-
tur an xp̄iam z baptizati fuissent. responderunt de xp̄o se ni-
chil hacte̅n̄ ut̅ audisse ut̅ sciuis-
se. Sic reuertentes panem unu̅
z caseum secu̅ retulerunt. ut̅
p̄ admirationem suis ostende-
quibꝰ. cibariis alienigene uesce-
rentur. ꝶorandum aut̅e cp̄
uiri cui ecclesiastica gaudent e-
munitate. z equos uiros ecclesiast̅i
eos uocant. q̄m̄q̄m laui z uxo-
rati comis cp̄ plongis trs hume-
rorum diffusis. solum armis re-
nuntiantes. in signum p̄techo-
nis pontifical impostuoe am-
plas i capite coronas bn̄t. Ic-
beni h̄ ab aliis diuisa minis z p̄-
ũsa. corporali tam mari qm̄ ca-
pitis signo q̄m̄ innuit. abn̄ut.
Renuit cp̄ quociens aliquibꝰ
abscessum includit. P̄tere
uiri in hac gente sedendo. mus-
eieī stando urinas emittunt.
ꞇam mulieres cp̄ qm̄ mares
diuaricatis cruribꝰ. ibiisꝗ; uir
cp̄ proten·s equitare solent. bn̄.

De clero hybine i multis lauda

Sed nunc ad cleri stilum
uertamur. Est autem
tire isti clerus satis religione z
mendabus. z inr̄ uarias cuibꝰ
posset uirtutes. castitans p̄o-
gatiua preminet z p̄cellit.
cem psalmis z horis lectionibꝰ

Adh aut̅e p̄ti-
alio popl̄o zeloti
p̄e uicio. laborat
hec natio.

Hec est copia cartarum dni Cristofori de Preston militis facte Anno H. Regis
secundi Massimo primo

Gomaneston

Indentura de convencionibz super adquisicione manij de Gomaneston p̄ H. de Preston
de H. de sco Amand. & Antiquio cart̄ penditz & munimentz &c.

Cest indente resmoigne q̄ come mons Aunmay de Seint Amant le piere & mons Robt de Preston soient
finalment acordez du bargain du manoir de Gomaneston oue les apptenances & oui ceo le dit
mons Aunmay eit p̄ ceo chartres grante au dit mons Robt deux rentes chartres lune de cissante
livrees & laute de trente livres a prendre de son dit manoir quens faitz sont trebblez & aussi eit paie
au dit mons Robt deuzo deners del une rente & seio deners del autre anno p̄ ses liez endentz
trebblez appert & aussint eit fait chartres de feffement du dit manoir au dit mons Robt & a ses
heirs & as entres p̄ luy nomez & ceo eit fait trebblez et aussint eit fait quatre liez dittones & a uns
gentes nomez p̄ le dit Robt p̄ la seisine de ceo & le les vint & quatre ages de terre vne acre de pree
dit James de Passelewe mist debat au dit mons Robt & ses compaignons deliverez et aussi en la
seisine le dit mons Robt & ses ditz compaignons luy eit fait trois releses de tout son droit du
dit manoir queux chartres faitz & les suseites le dit mons Aunmay ad fait enseallez en sa
presence demesne de son priue seal & les ad deliure au dit mons Robt et le dit mons Aunmay
ad pleinement receu du dit mons Robt toute la some dentre eux acordez quele il dust auoir p̄
le dit bargain et ouer ceo le dit mons Aunmay loialment empront de trauailler a la court le Roy et
en haste come il purra bonement a illoeques recouerer les deux chartres de rent charge & sa
charge de feffement & le releses susditz & les fera estre enroullez as costages du dit Robt
come en fees si leuer ses clercs Et aussi il empront loialment q̄ touz les anciennes chartres
munimentz cartes & remembrances touchantes le dit manoir q̄ sont deuers luy si nulles
uenoient il fera cercher oue tout sa haste quil purra & les fera deliuer au dit mons Robt sanz
delay Et aussint il empront loialment q̄ tant de foiz q̄ le dit mons Robt voudra couerter
nouelles rentes ou manoir auantdit tielles come le dit mons Aunmay luy ad fait auoir q̄ le
dit mons Aunmay les fera a luy faire sanz delay as costages du dit Robt. En tesmoignance
de queu chose a cestes liez endentz les auantditz mons Aunmay & Robt a cestes endentes ont
mys lour seals. don le mercredy lendemein de l'Assumpcion de nre dame l'an du regne nre
seign le Roy Edward tierz puis la conquest trenteseptisme

Indentura Almar̄ fil̄. R. Ad implendum couenciones part̄ sui fact de R. p. de Gomán
Ceste indente faite entre mons Aunmay de seint Amant le fitz & mons Robert   eston
de preston resmoigne q̄ come mons Aunmay de seint Amant le piere eut finalment

62 The Gormanston Register, 1397-98. (Ms 1646.)

The ancient register book of the Preston family of Gormanston, Co. Meath was compiled for the then lord of the manor, Sir Christopher de Preston, mainly in the period 1397-98. The family originated in Preston in Lancashire and acquired estates in Co. Meath early in the fourteenth century. The volume consists of transcripts of title deeds for de Preston properties and those of allied families, including de Bermingham, de Lacy, de Londres and FitzGerald. It is mainly in Latin but there are also a few items in English and in French. The deed shown here is in French and records the purchase of the manor of Gormanston by Robert de Preston, Chief Justice of Ireland, from Ammari de Seint Amant in 1363. The volume consists of 223 parchment folios; it is bound in oak boards covered in decorated calf. It was purchased in 1962.

The Preston coat of arms with the motto, *sans tache* (without stain).

63 An illuminated manuscript with a text by Franz von Retz, ***Defensorium Inviolatae Virginitatis Beatae Mariae,*** South-German, *c.* 1500. (9 x 7.5 cm; Ms 32,513.)

Franz von Retz (*c.* 1343-1427) was a Dominican theologian who taught at Vienna University. His text ('a defence of the inviolate virginity of Blessed Mary') is based on quotations from such authorities as Albertus Magnus, St Augustine and Isidore of Seville. It postulates various phenomena and strange occurrences as grounds for accepting the concept of the Virgin Birth. The volume consists of thirty-seven vellum folios, with a text in Latin and German on the verso of each folio and an associated painting on the recto. That reproduced here recalls a story from ancient Rome in which the maiden Claudia pulled a vessel ashore after it had gone aground in the Tiber. The text suggests that if such a strange occurrence took place, there is no reason why the Virgin should not have conceived and borne a child.

This manuscript copy is undated but the imagery, the style and the text indicate that it was produced in Germany around 1500. It was a popular work in the region of Austria and Bavaria, and fourteen manuscript copies of the text survive from the fifteenth century. Six *incunabula* (fifteenth-century printed books) also survive; as printing was common in Germany at the time, it is likely that this de-luxe manuscript volume in vellum was made for presentation purposes. It was expensively produced and has gold-leaf decoration; it was probably executed in a lay professional scriptorium.

With the change in religious and political climate which set in with the Reformation in the 1520s, this type of illustrated manuscript devoted to the Virgin Mary was no longer produced in Germany, which means that this is one of the last representatives of the genre.

Articles of Agreement made and concluded on this third day of February 1649 betweene y most Hon[oura]ble Oliver Cromwell Lord L[ieutenan]t Gen[era]ll of Ireland and [the] Col. [and] [Officers] [and] others Governo[rs] of y Towne of [Feather] concerning the surrender of y said Towne as followeth. viz:

1[st] [It]imes That all officers [and] so[ldiers] shall march freely with theire [horses] and Armes and all other Goods bagg [and] baggage [and] Cullours flying [and] [drums] beating [and] ball in bouch [and] [march] [away] [to] [a] place within his Ma[jes]ties quarters [and] [safely] convoy'd thither free from violence from any of the [Parliam]ts side.

2[nd] That all the Countrye [famelyes] [and] Inhabitants or others any of y [officers] [may] [keep] [and] enjoye theire goods, either in Towne or abroad [that] if they or any of them bee disposed to [settle] themselves to theire [former] [habitations] in y Country, that they [may] [have] liberty [and] privilege of theire [former] [that], [and] admittance to enjoye theire holding [paying] Contribution as others in y [Countrye] do, [and] to carrye with them safely such goods as they have within this [Garrison].

3rd That all the Clergiemen [and] [Ploughers] both of this [Towne] [and] [Country] now in this [Garrison] may freely march bagg and baggage without any annoyance or prejudice in body, or Goods.

4th That all and every the Inhabitants of the said Towne [with] their [wives] and Children [and] servants, with all theire goods and [Chattles] both within the Towne and abroad [in] the Country, shall [goe] [safe] from hind'ranc and all others [and] shall quietly [and] undisturbedly enjoye theire Estates both reall [and] personall in as free and as good A Condition as any English or Irish shall hold his or theire [Estates] in this [Kingdome], they and every [one] of them paying such Contributions as the rest of the [Inhabitants] [do] [freely] [of] [theire] Estates and no more.

In Consideration hereof the said Governo[r] doth hereby Engage himselfe that he will deliver upp the said Towne with all things therin (except such things s are before agreed upon to bee taken away with them) by eight of the clocke this morning

Cromwell

The Portrayture of his Excellency
The Right Honorable
OLIVER CROMWELL
Lord Governour of Ireland &c:
P:S exc:lit

64 Articles of agreement between Oliver Cromwell and Piers Butler for the surrender of Fethard, 3 February 1650. (Deed 7403.)

Cromwell landed in Dublin in August 1649, and by the end of the year had taken Drogheda, Wexford, New Ross and Carrick-on-Suir. His next object was to capture the rich Tipperary heartland and, in particular, to reduce the towns of Clonmel, Fethard, Cashel and Cahir. Fethard offered no resistance and surrendered on 3 February 1650 (1649 Old Style dating). Cromwell honoured his promise to show leniency to towns which surrendered without resistance and agreed generous terms. The garrison was allowed to march out under arms, and clergy were also free to leave the town. The officers and inhabitants were given the option of retaining their property without molestation or of going abroad with whatever personal effects they could carry.

The document was acquired with the papers of Captain C. R. Barton of Fethard which were donated in 1956.

Journal.

April 9:th 1772   I sailed from Deptford, but got no further than Woolwich where we were detained by Easterly Winds till the 22:d, when we fell down to Longreach and the next day was join'd by the Adventure. Here both Ships recieved on board their Powder, Guns, Gunner's Stores and Marines. —

May 10:th   We left Long-reach with orders to touch at Plymouth, but in flying down the River, the Resolution was found to be very crank, which made it very necessary to put into Sheerness, in order to remove this evil, by making some alterations in her upper-works, which the Officers of the Yard were order'd to take in hand immediately and Lord Sandwich and Sir Hugh Palliser came down to see that these things were done in such a manner as might effectually answer the purpose intended.

June 22:d   On the 22:d of June the Ship were again compleated for Sea, when I sailed from Sheerness and on the 3:d of July joined the Adventure in Plymouth Sound. The evening before we got off the Sound Lord Sandwich in the Augusta Yacht, (who was on his return from visiting the several Dock Yards) with the Glory Frigate and Hazard Sloop. We saluted His Lordship with Seventeen Guns, and soon after he and Sir Hugh Palliser gave us the last mark of the very great attention they had paid to this equipment, by coming on board to satisfy themselves that every thing was done to my wish and that the Ship was found to answer to my satisfaction. —

At Plymouth I received my instructions, dated the 25:th of June, directing me to take under my Command the Adventure Sloop; to make the best of my way to Madeira, there take in a supply of Wine and then proceed to the Cape of Good Hope, where I was to refresh the Ships
Companies

65 'A Journal of the Proceedings of His Majesty's Sloop the *Resolution* in a Voyage on Discoveries towards the South Pole and round the World, by Captain James Cook', 1772-75. (Joly Mss 7-8.)

There are a number of contemporary manuscript copies of the Journal of Cook's second voyage, most of which are in libraries and museums in England. In preparing the text for publication, Cook did a great deal of revision in successive drafts, and some of the manuscripts are in his hand and others are in the handwriting of clerks. This copy appears to be in the hand of the clerk who accompanied Cook on his third voyage. It may have been written in the course of preparing an edition of the work.

The scientists on Cook's expeditions collected specimens illustrating ethnography and flora and fauna. Specimens of bark cloth from the South Seas, claimed to have been brought back from these expeditions, are preserved in Joly Ms 9.

A

V O Y A G E

TOWARDS THE

S O U T H   P O L E,

AND

R O U N D   T H E   W O R L D.

BOOK I.

From our Departure from England, to leaving
the Society Ifles, the firft Time.

C H A P. I.

*Paffage from Deptford to the Cape of Good Hope, with an
Account of feveral Incidents that happened by the
Way, and Tranfactions there.*

I SAILED from Deptford, April 9th, 1772, but got no farther than Woolwich; where I was detained by eafterly winds till the 22d, when the fhip fell down to Long Reach, and the next day was joined by the Adventure.' Here both fhips received on board their powder, guns, gunner's ftores, and marines.

1772.
April.

VOL. 1.   B   On

66 An illuminated address presented to Charles Stewart Parnell on his return from the United States, March 1880. (90 x 63 cm; Ms 22,028.)

In December 1879 the Land League dispatched Parnell and John Dillon to the United States to collect funds for the relief of distress in the west of Ireland. Parnell addressed meetings at over sixty venues and raised more than £70,000. While the more extreme Fenians were hostile, John Devoy and Clan na Gael supported the tour. Due to the intervention of influential Irish-Americans, he was granted the rare privilege of addressing the United States Congress on 2 February 1880. In his speech he concentrated on the land situation and the current distress in Ireland and he proposed that the landlords be bought out, if necessary by compulsion. The historic occasion is depicted in an illuminated address presented to him by the Land League on his return to Ireland. The address was executed by Thomas J. Lynch, a Dublin artist.

Address to
Chas S. Parnell, Esq.

President of the Irish National Land League.

Sir, We tender you on behalf of the tenant farmers of Ireland a hearty *Cead Mile Failte* Home again to the country you have so nobly served during your brief sojourn in the United States. Short as your stay has been in that mighty Western Republic it has nevertheless been signalised by the most splendid and opportune services to the present wants of our starving people, while being at the same time pregnant with encouraging hope for the future welfare of our fatherland. While thousands of families, pauperised through the operation of an infamous land system have been saved by your wondrous and indefatigable exertions from the fate which befel our famine-slaughtered kindred in '47 and '48, the heart of Ireland has followed in the wake of your triumphal progress among a generous and sympathetic people, and throbbed with expectant joy as they pledged you the moral support of America in our struggle against felonious landlordism.

As the representative of the Irish People and delegate of the National Land League, you and your colleague Mr. John Dillon, have had extended to you honours and manifestations of encouragement surpassing any yet conferred by the land of Washington Franklin and Carroll upon the champions of oppressed nationalities; and your country felt proudly raised once more to the dignity of a recognised nation when the House of Representatives bestowed upon you the proud privilege of advocating the cause of Ireland before the most representative assembly of the greatest Government in the world. From the St Lawrence to the Potomac - from the Atlantic seaboard to the plains of Minnesota - the landlord-banished portion of our people have pledged anew their fidelity to Ireland and their vows for her deliverance, when by those enthusiastic greetings immense demonstrations and military parades they welcomed you as the ambassador of their suffering stricken land while their munificent contributions and promised continued cooperation infuses a spirit of sanguine expectation into our impoverished people that the fell cause of their poverty and humiliation will soon fall beneath the united efforts of our entire race.

You are landing in Ireland at a time which may be deemed a momentous period in the history of that coercive and infamous Union which has been such a political scourge to our country and when the spirit of Irish nationality is endangered by the virulent attacks of a truculent and unscrupulous Government. We sincerely hope that you have sped across the waters like another Perseus to save the Andromeda of nations from the political monster now threatening her with national destruction and that her deliverance from immediate danger achieved you will return to the assistance of your colleagues to complete the mission you were sent on by the body of which you are the honoured and trusted Head.

Signed,

Patrick Egan	J. F. Grehan	Thomas Sexton
A. J. Kettle	R. J. Donnelly	Michael Davitt

PARNELL ADDRESSING THE UNITED STATES HOUSE OF REPRESENTATIVES IN SESSION.
WASHINGTON, FEBY 2ND 1880.

Designed & Painted by T. J. Lynch, 34 Middle Abbey St. Dublin.

An Unsocial Socialist.

By George Bernard Shaw.

Chapter I

In the dusk of an October evening, a sensible looking woman of ~~could~~ forty ~~illegible~~ came out through an oaken door upon a broad landing on the first floor of an old English country house. Her hair had fallen forward as if she had been stooping over book or pen, and she stood for a moment to smooth it, and to gaze contemplatively — not in the least sentimentally — through the tall, narrow window. The sun was setting, but its glories were at the other side of the house; for this window looked eastward, where the landscape of sheepwalks and pasture lands was sobering at the approach of darkness.

The lady, like one to whom silence and quiet were ~~illegible~~ luxuries, lingered on the landing for some time. Then she turned towards another door, on which was the inscription, in white letters, <u>Class Room No 6.</u> Arrested in the act of entering by some whispering above, she paused in the doorway, and looked up, her sight led by the stairs, a broad smooth handrail which, sweeping round in an unbroken curve at each landing, formed an inclined plane from the top to the bottom of the house.

A young voice, apparently mimicking that of some music mistress, now came from above, saying,

"We will take the <u>Études de la Velocité</u> next, if you please, ladies."

Immediately a girl in a white dress shot down through space, whirled round the curve with a fearless centrifugal toss of her ankle, ~~illegible~~

67 The George Bernard Shaw manuscripts: *An Unsocial Socialist.* (Ms 850.)

In April 1945, Dr R. J. Hayes, Director of the National Library, wrote a brief note to Shaw stating: 'I can think of no more appropriate place than the National Library of Ireland for the permanent preservation for posterity of your manuscripts, correspondence and first editions. Can you?' Shaw replied from London: 'Your invitation as National Librarian is in the nature of a command . . . I am having them tidied up and bound; and when this is finished you shall have them . . .'

The manuscripts acquired were those of *The Irrational Knot* (1883), *Cashel Byron's Profession* (1886), *An Unsocial Socialist* (1887), *Immaturity* (1930), and *An Unfinished Novel* (1958) – the dates refer to year of publication.

G.BERNARD SHAW.

Preliminary Meeting

At a meeting held on Monday, 13 July 1893, at 9 Lower O'Connell street, Dublin. Douglas Hyde LL.D. in the chair, the following also present.

Chas Percy Bushe   John McNeill BA

Jas Michl Cogan   Patrick O'Brien.

Thos W Ellerker   T. O'Neill Russell.

Rev. Wm Hayden S.J.   Fitzgerald?

Patrick J Hogan. M.A.

Martin Kelly

It was moved by J McNeill   seconded by J Mc Cogan and resolved

That a Society be formed under the name of the Gaelic League for the purpose of keeping the Irish Language spoken in Ireland.

Moved by T O'Neill Russell, seconded by M Kelly and resolved unanimously.

That we here present constitute ourselves ~~the~~ a Society under the name and for the purpose aforesaid

68 The first Gaelic League minute book, July 1893-June 1896. (Ms 19, 315.)

The Gaelic League was established in Dublin on 31 July 1893 at a meeting convened by Eoin MacNeill. It was held at 9 Lower O'Connell Street where Martin Kelly worked as a civil service tutor. A preliminary meeting was held first (wrongly dated in the minutes) and then the inaugural meeting. The minutes of the inaugural meeting are very brief and the only business recorded was the formation of 'the Committee or Council of the Gaelic League'. The minute book was acquired in 1975; the Library also has a number of minute books of various committees of Conradh na Gaeilge, as the organisation has been known for most of its life.

The premises of Conradh na Gaeilge in Sackville (O'Connell) Street at the turn of the century. (*An Claidheamh Soluis*, 3 April 1901.)

153

Pearse surrendering to General Lowe who is accompanied by his staff officer, Major de Courcey Wheeler (near camera). (*Daily Sketch*, 10 May 1916.)

69 The record of the decision by the Republican forces to enter negotiations with the British, 29 April 1916. (Ms 15,453.)

On Friday, 28 April 1916, the fifth day of the Easter Rising, the Republican forces evacuated the General Post Office in O'Connell Street. The following morning, the Commander-in-Chief, Patrick Pearse, and other leaders met at 16 Moore Street, a fish shop. Their decision to enter negotiations was recorded on a sheet of cardboard, possibly the only writing material to hand. The document was found by the householders when they returned after hostilities ceased. It was purchased by the Library in 1967. It reads:

H. Q. Moore St
Believing that the glorious stand which has been made by the soldiers of Irish freedom during the past five days in Dublin has been sufficient to gain recognition of Ireland's national claim at an international peace conference, and desirous of preventing further slaughter of the civil population and to save the lives of as many as possible of our followers, the Members of the Provisional Government here present have agreed by a majority to open negotiations with the British commander.

29 April 1916.

P. H. Pearse,
Comandant General,
Commanding [?] in Chief,
Army of the Irish Republic.

H.Q. Moore St.

Believing that the glorious
stand which has been made
by the soldiers of Irish freedom during the past five
days in Dublin has been sufficient to gain recognition of
Ireland's claim at an
international peace conference, and
desirous of preventing further
slaughter of the civil population,
and to save the lives of as
many as possible of our followers,
the members of the Provisional Government here present have agreed
by a majority to open negotiations with the British Commander.

P. H. Pearse,
Commandant General,
Commanding in Chief
Army of the Irish Republic.

29 April 1916

But it spring to summer wears
This being round october twent'

[deleted lines]
Great windows open to the south)

a Georgian house under a hill
[deleted lines]
Two girls in silk kimonos, both

Beautiful, on a gazell
She [deleted] serpentine — [deleted]
[deleted]

shape/ The [deleted]
[deleted] condemn to death She
[deleted] elects drag out their years
conspiring among the ignorant

[deleted lines]
about [deleted] dream. The abstraction of a dream
Her body grown skeleton gaunt —
a [deleted] symbol of it tell of her politics
many a time I think to seek
one or the other out
of that old georgian h[ouse]
[deleted] memory [deleted]

[deleted]
[deleted]
memo[ry] of [deleted]
[deleted]
[deleted]
Beautiful on [deleted]

In Memory of Eva Gore - Booth & Con Markievicz
The light of evening, Lissadell
a Georgian house under a hill
Great windows open to the south,
Two girls in silk kimonos, both
Beautiful, one a gazell
But the spring to summer wears —
The [deleted] is condemn to death;
Pardon [deleted] Drag out lonely years
Conspiring among the ignorant
The [deleted] dream under all things seem
the abstraction of a dream
Her body grown skeleton gaunt
the [deleted] of her politics
many a time I think to seek
one or the other out & speak
Of that old georgian mansion, mix
Pictures of the mind, recall
that table & the talk of youth
Two girls in silk kimonos, both
Beautiful, one a gazell.
New shadows [deleted]
Do they know what living meant

IN MEMORY OF EVA GORE BOOTH
AND CON MARKIEWICZ

·⋯✦ I ✦⋯·

The light of evening, Lissadell,
Great windows open to the south,
Two girls in silk kimonos, both
Beautiful, one a gazelle.
But a raving autumn shears
Blossom from the summer's wreath;
The older is condemned to death,
Pardoned, drags out lonely years
Conspiring among the ignorant.
I know not what the younger dreams—
Some vague Utopia—and she seems,
When withered old and skeleton-gaunt,
An image of such politics.

70 The Yeats Papers: drafts of a poem by W. B. Yeats. (Ms 30,149.)

This well-known poem was first published in 1929 in *The Winding Stair*. The subjects were the daughters of Sir Henry Gore-Booth of Lissadell, Co. Sligo. These remarkable women were Eva Gore-Booth (1870-1926), a published poet and trades union activist in Manchester; and the Countess Constance Markievicz (1868-1927), a celebrated figure in the Irish revolutionary movement who was sentenced to death for her part in the 1916 Rising but had her sentence commuted.

Most of the manuscripts of W. B. Yeats are now held by the National Library. They were donated by the poet's family in 1958, 1964 and 1985.

VIII. GAELIC MANUSCRIPTS

The collection of Gaelic manuscripts now amounts to approximately 1,200 items. Most are bound volumes but some of the more recent consist of folders of loose papers. As many of the bound volumes include several different texts the collection represents a very extensive corpus of literature. The older manuscripts are vellum or parchment but from about the sixteenth century paper gradually takes over. They are almost all in that distinctive pointed script which was developed in the sixth and seventh centuries exclusively for texts in the Irish language and is still used by some people.

In terms of period, the manuscripts range from the fourteenth to the twentieth century. The contents, however, span a longer period of time as many include copies of earlier manuscripts. The most notable example is Ms G50, a seventeenth-century paper manuscript which includes the poems of the eighth-century monk Blathmac (pronounced blathmhac – blávoc). Apart from its great linguistic and literary interest, this text provides unique information on the nature of the cult of the Virgin Mary in the eighth century. As no other copy of the text has survived, the importance of this relatively late exemplar is obvious and well illustrates the nature of manuscript tradition.

The National Library collection is generally representative of the surviving corpus of Irish literature, lore and history generated by scholars and transmitted by scribes down through the ages. It includes many examples of that ancient genre of imaginative literature which celebrates the gods and goddesses of Celtic mythology and the heroic deeds of such legendary figures as Cú Chulainn, the Red Branch Knights, Oisín and the Fianna. The bardic tradition and the form of the medieval praise-poem are particularly well represented in that the Library has the earliest surviving example of a book of praise poetry, the fourteenth-century *duanaire* of Tomás Mág Shamhradháin of Tullyhaw, Co. Cavan, known as the Book of Magauran. The modern period is also well covered as the collection includes much of the prose and poetry from the seventeenth to the nineteenth century. Among the writers represented are Aodhagán Ó Rathaille, Peadar Ó Doirnín, Eoghan Ruadh Ó Súilleabháin and Brian Merriman. Their texts were copied and recopied many times over the years; they are preserved with varying degrees of accuracy in a large number of manuscripts.

The fields of scholarship other than literature represented in the collection include genealogy, the hagiography of Irish saints, religion and *dinnseanchas* (place-lore). There are a number of legal texts, some of which incorporate 'Brehon' law and later accretions reflecting contemporary practice. Especially important are the relatively large number of medical manuscripts. These date from the fifteenth century onwards, and are mainly translations of Latin texts imported from Britain and the Continent.

A peculiar feature of Irish manuscript tradition is that the bulk of the manuscripts date from the period when printing was widely available, but apart from religious matter such as bibles or catechisms few Irish texts appeared in print. The failure to publish Irish texts was partly due to the difficult political situation of the Irish-speaking community from the seventeenth century onwards, but the main reason was probably commercial. There may not have been enough people literate in Irish to warrant the expense of publication; the minority committed to Irish had to rely on professional scribes to provide them with texts.

The manuscript tradition was particularly strong in Munster, north Connacht, north Leinster and south-east Ulster; it was also strong in Belfast and in Dublin which had a large concentration of scribes. Among the more prominent of those located in Dublin in the eighteenth century were Seán Ó Neachtain and his son Tadhg, Muiris Ó Gormáin and the Catholic archbishop, John Carpenter. A large number were also active in Co. Cork, of whom the most notable were members of the Ó Longáin family. Some of the scribes were also teachers and many combined the transcribing of texts with tutoring when it was available.

From the seventeenth century onwards there have been many active collectors of Irish manuscripts. Some were specifically concerned with preserving the language and culture, while others were interested in antiquarian studies in general. In any case, collections were built up and preserved, and many of them have since found their way to the National Library. The first major accession was in 1907 when the executors of the celebrated Irish scholar, David Comyn, presented his collection of thirty-six manuscripts. The most notable acquisition, however, was in 1931 when the National Library purchased 178 volumes from the great library assembled at Cheltenham by Sir Thomas Phillipps. Among the items acquired were vellum manuscripts from the fourteenth century, rare Ulster tales, medical and legal texts, and the only surviving copy of the *Poems of Blathmac* mentioned above. Another important accession was the gift in 1944 of ninety manuscripts from the collection of the Dublin scholar and civil servant, Séamus Ó Casaide, who is considered to have been the last of the great collectors of Irish manuscripts. Hundreds of individual items have also, of course, been acquired by purchase or donation over the years.

More than any of the other types of material in the National Library, the Gaelic manuscripts show signs of their age and of the circumstances in which they were copied, studied, stored and passed down over the centuries. They are often battered and tattered, well-worn, and discoloured and stained from smoke, sweat, damp and grime. But their condition is relatively immaterial; what matters is that they have survived and now represent an entire national literary and cultural heritage.

In any consideration of the National Library's Gaelic manuscripts tribute must be paid to the great Irish scholar, Nessa Ní Shéaghdha, of the School of Celtic Studies at the Dublin Institute for Advanced Studies, who died in April 1993. Her detailed catalogues covering approximately half the collection have been published in a series of fascicles since 1961. Members of staff of the National Library are among the many with whom she most generously shared her immense knowledge of Irish manuscript tradition over the years.

The Library at Thirlestaine House, Cheltenham, with Thomas Fitzroy Fenwick, a descendant of Sir Thomas Phillipps, who negotiated the sale of the Gaelic manuscripts to the National Library. (A. N. L. Munby, *The Dispersal of the Phillipps Library,* Cambridge University Press, 1960.)

161

71 Duanaire Mhéig Shamhradháin or The Book of Magauran (MacGovern);
fourteenth century. (31 x 22 cm; Ms G1200.)

This is a vellum manuscript consisting of poems written in praise of the family of
Tomás Mág Shamhradháin (1303-1343), chief of Teallach nEacach (Tullyhaw) in
Co. Cavan. In the Middle Ages many reigning families had a similar collection
(*duanaire*) of bardic poetry, but few have survived and this is now the earliest and
most important example. It was acquired by the Library in 1972 from the O'Conor
Don family at Clonalis, Co. Roscommon, in whose possession it had been for
centuries.

The page shown here is in the hand of Ruaidhrí Ó Cianáin, the main scribe of the
volume. It includes the beginning of a poem by Tadhg Mór Ó hUiginn (died 1315?)
describing his distress on hearing news of the murder of Brían Mág Shamhradháin,
father of Tomás. The foul deed was perpetrated by Aodh Bréifneach Ó Conchubhair
and the Clan Muircheartaigh (Í Chonchbhair). It begins with the large initial in the
second column and reads:

A fhir táinig re tásg mBriain,
tugais mhise fa mhóirchiaigh;
mh'ucht ó sgeol an táisg is teinn
mo dheor do fháisg óm incheinn.

O thou who hast come with the bad news of Brian,
thou hast overwhelmed me with gloom;
sore is my breast at the sad tidings;
it has pressed out tears from my brain.
(Edited text and translation by Lambert McKenna; D.I.A.S. 1947).

The library at Clonalis, a watercolour by Alison, Lady Rosse, now in the National
Library.

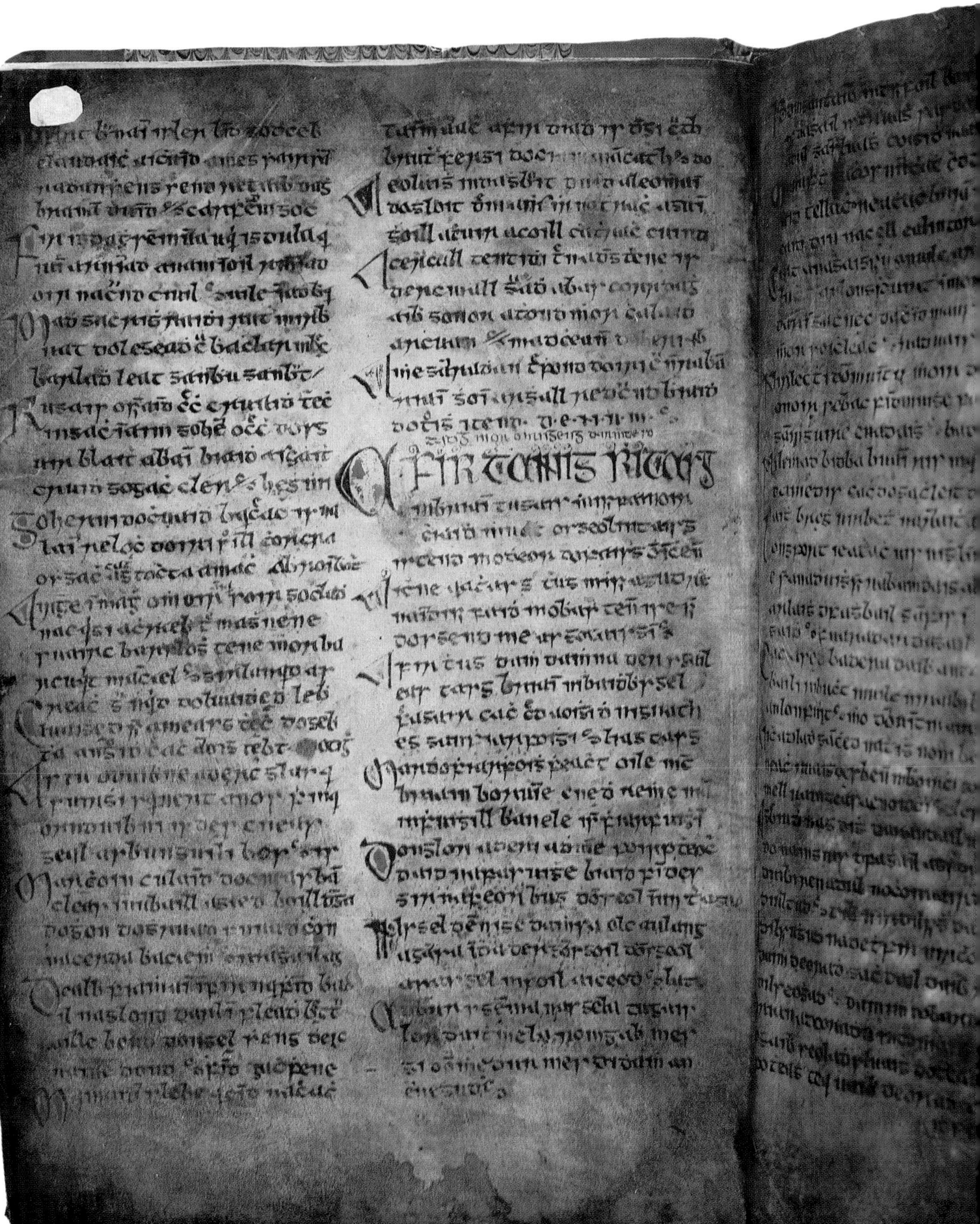

72 A fourteenth- or fifteenth-century vellum manuscript with an illuminated miniature of Noah's Ark. (20 x 13 cm; Ms G3; formerly Phillipps.)

Illustrations are extremely rare in Gaelic manuscripts, which makes this specimen all the more interesting. The manuscript in which it occurs, Ms G3, was acquired by the scholar and antiquary, Edward O'Reilly (*c.* 1765-1830), along with Ms G2, which was originally part of the same volume but became detached. They were later acquired by John O'Donovan and eventually passed to the Phillipps Library at Cheltenham; they were among the items purchased by the National Library in 1931. The two volumes seem to be mainly in the hand of Adhamh Ó Cianáin, whose death at Lisgool, Co. Fermanagh, is recorded in the Annals of the Four Masters for 1373; he may have been a relative of Ruaidhrí Ó Cianáin, the scribe of the Book of Magauran. The contents include historical and genealogical texts and some law and grammar.

Noah's Ark is often featured in continental manuscripts of the period. This example shows the compartments for Noah's family, the horses and the birds. It is headed 'Denamh na hairce andseo 7 Sliabh Armenia fuithe' (the construction of the Ark with the Armenian mountain below). It occurs between items relating to Fionn Mac Cumhaill and Solomon.

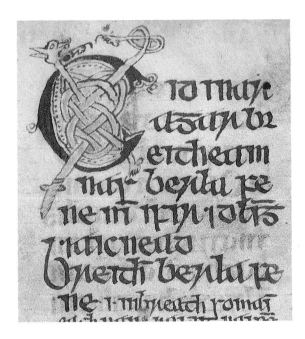

165

73 The seventeenth-century paper manuscript with **the poems of the eighth-century monk Blathmac.** (20 x 15 cm; Ms G50; formerly Phillipps.)

Although this manuscript was written in the seventeenth century and is on paper, in general character its language is strict Old Irish (from about the eighth century). This is particularly exciting for scholars, as much of the extant material from this early period consists only of fragmentary glosses and here they find a substantial quantity of continuous text. The poems do not appear in any other source and none of them seem to derive from any surviving manuscript. It has been argued that the exemplar from which this manuscript was transcribed was the lost twelfth-century codex, the 'Book of Glendalough'.

Blathmac has been identified as a son of Cú Brettan who is mentioned in the saga of the Battle of Allen and whose death is recorded in the Annals of Ulster in the year 739 A.D. (= 740). Blathmac himself, from the evidence of the poems, was probably a monk and had received the normal ecclesiastical training of his day. He would have been familiar with the scriptures and also with some apocryphal texts; his formation would also probably have involved training in the composition of Irish verse. As mentioned in the introduction to this chapter, Blathmac's poems are an important source of information on the cult of the Virgin Mary in the eighth century. The poems begin on line three of the page shown here.

Blathmac mac Con Bretan Maic Conguso do Feraibh Rois do-rigni in ndúthracht-sa do Mairi 7 dia mac.
It is Blathmac son of Cú Brettan son of Congus of the Fir Rois has made this devoted offering to Mary and her son.

Tair cucum, a Maire boíd
do choíniuth frit do rochoím;
dirsan dul fri croich dot mac
ba mind már, ba masgérat.

Come to me, loving Mary,
that I may keen with you your very dear one.
Alas that your son should go to the cross,
he who was a great diadem, a beautiful hero.

(Edited text and translation by James Carney; Irish Texts Society, 1964).

166

74 A volume of poems in the hand of John Carpenter, Archbishop of Dublin; 1744-5. (20 x 15 cm; Ms G82; formerly Phillipps.)

Throughout the eighteenth century there was an active circle of scholars, scribes, patrons and owners of Gaelic manuscripts in Dublin. One of the most prominent was John Carpenter (Sea[a]n Macat[s]ao[i]r), a native of the city and the son of a merchant-tailor. He was educated at Lisbon and served as a priest in Dublin until his appointment as Catholic archbishop in 1770.

168

This is one of two manuscripts transcribed by Carpenter held by the Library. Most of the poems seem to be of northern origin. The page shown here has the beginning of a long poem entitled 'Comhrán Duine agas an Bháis' (a conversation between a Person and Death) which may be translated as:

Person.   Who is that yonder approaching me?
                in the form of a robber prowling by night,
                a sharpened axe in his right hand,
                an hour-glass in his left hand.

Death.   I am Death, don't be startled,
                your time in this life is brief,
                you will ride on a fine bier,
                [?] going to the churchyard to join your fellows.

75 Illuminated address presented to Douglas Hyde by a New York branch of Conradh na Gaeilge, 26 November 1905. (72 x 55 cm; Ms 22,029.)

Dr Douglas Hyde, President of Conradh na Gaeilge, toured the United States on a promotional and fund-raising mission in the period from November 1905 to June 1906. He travelled to most of the cities with large Irish populations and raised over £10,000. The address on vellum was designed by Éoin S. Ua Liaigh and presented at a function in Carnegie Hall in New York. Hyde describes the occasion in his account of the tour, *Mo Thuras go hAmerice* (1937); a form of his pen–name *An Craoibhín Aoibhinn* (the delightful little branch) appears on the cover of the book. Dr Hyde was the first President of Ireland and held the office for the period 1937-45.

Seachtmhain ó'n lá-so, do bhí beirt againn pósta. Tomás ó Criomhthain, agus Máire ní Catháin, sa t-seachtmhain deireannach d'Inid .1878.

Níor lá go tí é, ar an "m'Buailtín", áit lonnaighthe na Sagairt, bhí ceithre fhichid ann, 7 do bhí tamall is gach tigh aca nuair go raibh an lá meall go maith, Do bhí an t-sráid-bhaile lán do dhaoine, mar do bhí a lán póstaí eile ann.

Do bhí ceithre bheidhleadóir ann, fear is gach tigh, á mealladh na bhfear isteach, 7 do bhí fear eile aca ná raibh in aon tigh, ach a g'ceann na

162 sráide, 7 níor bh'é an fear ba measa do bhí díolta é, mar ba lasmuich do bhí an Sluagh,

Do b'éigeadar dúinn Sgaramaint leis an m'Buailtín sa deire, ansan n'som ba mhó go raibh greann ann, ach ó ba rud é go raibh an fharraige mór roimhe, 7 cuid mhaith againn le tabhairt isteach, do bhí an oidhche ana bhreágh 7 mórán anuich, bád mhóra, do bhí anuairí-sin ann do tugadh mórán leo.

Do lean mórán ó'n áit anuich sin, daoine muinnteartha, do bhí ainnsin fhliuchráiseach 7 rinnce ar siubhal 7 gach eile greann fhaoileadh dighe, 7 bídh, go headarshuth amáireach, Do bhailibh muinn-tir na Tíorach leó, 7 do bhí an t-iomlán imighthe,

Dubhairt daoine go raibh cúig bliadhna déag roimhe-sin ó phós oiread san bliadhain áinsin.

Do bhí obair 7 gnó ar siubhal an chuid eile do'n m'bliadhain, bliadhain mhór éisg do b'eadh an bhliadhain sa-sion anuas, ní raibh mairicréil, ná gleasaidh ar siubhal, ach iasc do bhí á marbhú ansa lá, le bád-mhóra 7 saidhne móra is gach bád aca, 7 fheirmeoirí na tuatha á cionnach uatha, 7 ó h-ocht go réilt, do sgillinní an céad air.

76 The manuscript of *An t-Oileánach* by Tomás Ó Criomhthain, 1920s. (Mainly 33 x 21 cm; Ms G1020.)

Tomás Ó Criomhthain (1856-1937), the youngest of six children, was born on An Blascaod Mór (Great Blasket Island), off the coast of Co. Kerry. His schooling began when he was ten years old and continued intermittently until he was eighteen. Irish, however, was not on the curriculum and it was only years later that he taught himself to read and write his native language. Brian Ó Ceallaigh, an Irish-language scholar from Killarney, persuaded Tomás to record life as lived on the islands. The record took the form of foolscap pages posted at regular intervals to Ó Ceallaigh, and later to An Seabhac (Pádraig Ó Siochfhradha). The first part of this record was published in book form in 1928 with the title *Allagar na h-Inise* (*Island Cross-Talk*). It was followed in 1929 by the autobiographical An t-Oileánach (*The Islandman,* translation by Robin Flower 1934). Due to their popularity and sociological importance, both the Irish and English versions were re-issued many times.

In the page reproduced here, Tomás recalls the day of his wedding; it took place in the last week of Shrovetide 1878 in Baile an Fheirtéaraigh (Ballyferriter) on the mainland, as there was no resident priest on the island. The last inhabitants of the Blaskets moved out in the 1950s and the islands which once supported a lively community are now deserted.

IX. MAPS

From a nucleus of 20,000 maps acquired with the RDS Library and the Joly Library in 1877, the collection of maps has grown to approximately 150,000 items. While many of the maps relate to Britain, Europe and the world at large, the collection is essentially Irish. It is a major source of information on the physical landscape and on features such as settlement, communications and land usage, particularly for the past four hundred years.

While the earliest map in the collection, a coloured sketch map of Europe, appears in a twelfth-century copy of the *Topographia Hiberniae* of Giraldus Cambrensis, there seems to have been neither a Norman nor a native Irish tradition of cartography, and there are no other notable maps until the period of the Tudor conquest in the sixteenth century. The Tudor monarchs required reliable maps for the purposes of strategic planning and the allocation of conquered territory; official cartographers were set to work in the wake of the armies. Prominent among these were Francis Jobson in Munster and Richard Bartlett in Ulster who are both represented in the Library's collection. Many of Bartlett's maps are in the form of bird's-eye views of towns and fortifications and are closer to the art of the engineer than that of the cartographer. Among the many other examples of the work of military engineers are the manuscript plans of towns and fortifications drawn by Captain Thomas Phillips for James II in 1685, and a volume of plans prepared by the Huguenot engineer, John Goubet, who served here with the Williamite army in 1690 and for some time afterwards.

Plans for colonisation followed the Tudor conquest, and the Library has some notable specimens of maps produced as part of the process of settlement. Most striking is the map of Mogeely, Co. Cork, part of the estate which Sir Walter Raleigh secured following the suppression of the Desmond rebellion in 1583. Of more general interest, however, are the maps arising from the Cromwellian confiscation of the 1650s which provide detailed coverage of much of Leinster, Munster and Connacht. These detailed barony and parish maps were produced by a team of 1,000 men under the direction of an Englishman, Sir William Petty. His system of plotting down the data in map form resulted in the survey becoming known as the Down Survey. While most of the original maps were lost in fires, the Library has acquired a set of coloured eighteenth-century copies of the majority.

The eighteenth century was a period of relative political stability in which the landed estates acquired in the preceding centuries generally prospered. The proprietors tended to regard maps as necessary aids to efficient administration, and land surveying became a flourishing profession. While almost all the maps produced in previous centuries were by foreigners, Irishmen now became prominent and their names are recorded on thousands of manuscript

175

estate maps. The earlier maps are in a rather minimalist style, but in the second half of the century the more artistic 'French' style was popularised by two French Huguenot cartographers, John Rocque and Bernard Scalé. This style featured decorative cartouches and a delicate use of colour differentiating land usage. The Library has built up a collection of estate maps representing over three hundred estates, most of which were acquired with collections of estate papers. A particularly notable accession was the gift in 1908 of 4,000 file copies of estate maps produced by the Dublin firm of surveyors, Brownrigg, Longfield and Murray. This unique archive was generated in the period 1775-1833 and includes material for most counties.

Another source of maps in the late eighteenth and early nineteenth centuries were the grand juries which exercised some of the functions of present-day county councils. Most of them commissioned printed maps of their counties for the purpose of promoting local development. The grand jury maps are usually on a scale of one or two inches to the mile and include physical features, administrative divisions, roads and important buildings. Detailed plans of cities and towns also became common in this period. The above-mentioned John Rocque was one of the most remarkable of the urban cartographers; he is best known for his magnificent four-sheet *Exact Survey of the City and Suburbs of Dublin* (1756). The Library has copies of most of the printed county and town maps. It also has a unique set of 202 coloured manuscript maps of mail-coach roads from the period 1805-16 which were deposited by the Commissioners of Public Works.

A feature of the maps produced in the eighteenth and early nineteenth centuries is their great variety. Each cartographer or map-maker was a law unto himself, and the maps tended to vary in style, scale and content. Greater standardisation was obviously desirable; when the government required detailed maps as a basis for a general valuation of land and houses in the 1820s, it commissioned the Ordnance Survey to produce printed maps of the entire country on a standard scale of six inches to the mile. The project was completed by 1846 and resulted in a total of 1906 sheets, each measuring three feet by two feet and representing twenty-four square miles. With such a large scale it was possible to show all houses in ground-plan and also such features as minor roads and field boundaries. The Ordnance Survey afterwards carried out a number of other complete surveys in various scales. Its extremely accurate and detailed maps were adequate for most purposes; they became the basis for official maps required for civil administration and projects such as roads and railways, and they replaced the traditional estate maps. The Library has a fairly comprehensive collection of Ordnance Survey maps; nowadays they are acquired in the medium of microfiche.

Finally, the Library has a good collection of general maps of Ireland from the late sixteenth century onwards, many of them in printed atlases. Most reflect the detailed surveying and mapping taking place at local level. For instance, the work of the Tudor surveyors is reflected in the general maps of Mercator, Ortelius and John Speed. The data acquired in the course of the Down Survey afterwards enabled William Petty to compile the first general map of Ireland (1685) which appears accurate to the eye. However, it was only with the very high standards of the Ordnance Survey almost two hundred years later that a really definitive map of Ireland was eventually achieved.

Land surveyors from a manuscript map of lands at Lislee, Co. Cork, by John Moloney, 1801; the instruments are the short chain and a circumferentor, a form of compass used for establishing angles relative to magnetic north. (15.B.14.)

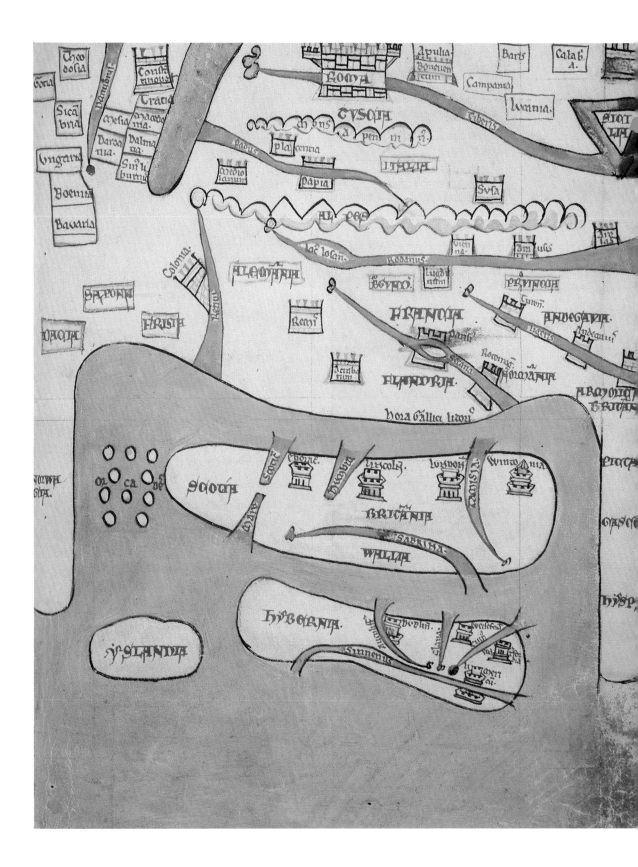

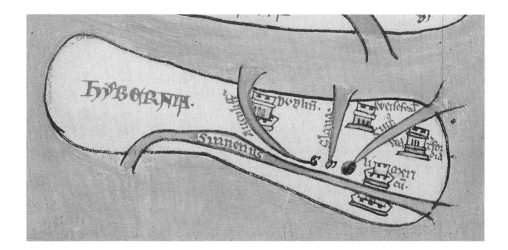

77 A map of Europe in a *c.* 1200 A.D. copy of Giraldus Cambrensis, *Topographia Hiberniae* – see no. 61. (Ms 700.)

The *Topographia Hiberniae,* a description of Ireland and its inhabitants, includes this schematic map, the earliest in the Library's collection. The sources of the map are European rather than Norman and it was probably copied from a contemporary *mappa mundi* (map of the world). The coverage of Ireland, however, is largely confined to the area of Norman influence; the map may be taken as representing in general terms the contemporary Norman understanding of the country.

Scotland, England and Wales, Iceland and Ireland are framed between Norway, to the left, and Spain and the South of France, to the right. The Liffey, Slaney, Suir and Shannon are shown with their ports: Dublin, Wexford, Waterford and Limerick, all of which were Norman centres. The Shannon and the Erne appear as one river, a confusion probably arising from the fact that their sources are in the same general area; the confusion suggests that the North-west was not well documented in the cartographer's sources. Detail is also limited for the neighbouring island where the only cities or towns to appear are York, Lincoln, London and Winchester.

The map may have originated as a guide for travellers from England to Rome. The route probably led via the Seine and Paris, across the Rhone at Lyon, across the Alps to Pavia, and from there to Piacenza and Rome.

78 Abraham Ortelius, *Theatrum Orbis Terrarum,* Antwerp, 1592 edition.

This celebrated atlas of the world includes the map of Ireland reproduced here. In the second half of the sixteenth century various Dutch cartographers availed of land surveys carried out during the Tudor conquest to produce reasonably accurate general maps of Ireland. This example, entitled in translation, 'A new map of the Britannic island of Ireland', was first published by Ortelius in the 1573 edition of his atlas. It was based on a large wall map of England, Scotland, Wales and Ireland published by Gerard Mercator at Duisburg in Germany in 1564. The Ortelius version became extremely popular and appeared in a number of editions.

The map was engraved and afterwards coloured by hand. The outline of the country is typical of the printed maps of the period which generally lagged behind contemporary cartographical knowledge. It indicates the territories of the major lords and chieftains, and includes towns, ecclesiastical sites and castles. Ulster was still unconquered and unexplored by English surveyors and as a result relatively little detail is given.

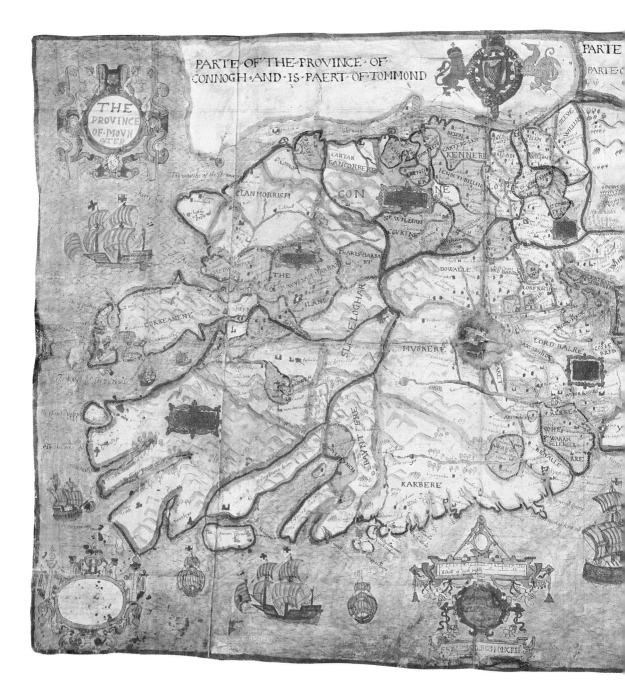

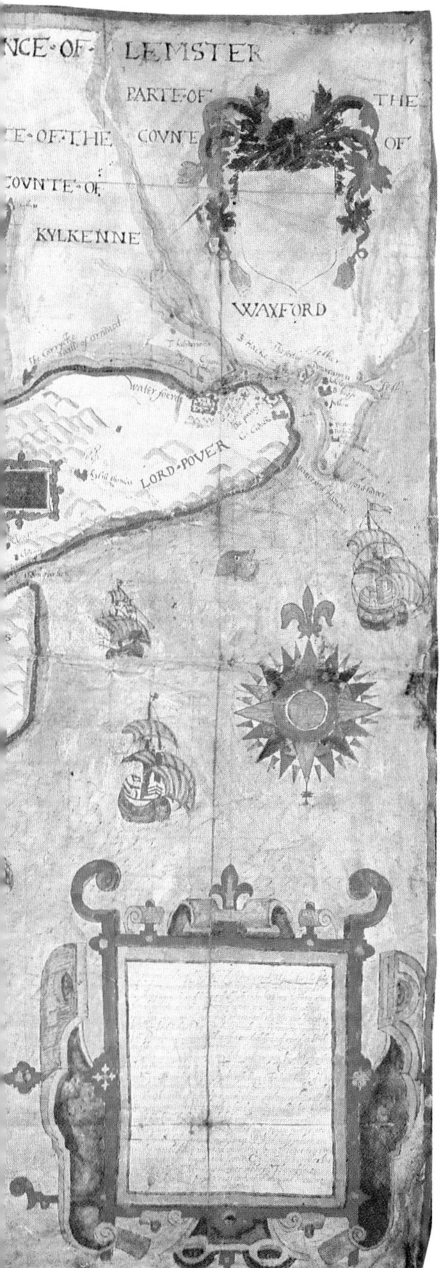
PARTE·OF
COVNTE
THE
OF
KYLKENNE
WAXFORD
LORD·POVER

79 A manuscript map by Francis Jobson, **'The Province of Mounster'**, *c.* 1592. (70 x 105 cm; 16.B.13.)

This manuscript map is painted on vellum. It was produced by Francis Jobson, an Englishman employed as a plantation surveyor in Munster for a period from 1586 onwards. Following the suppression of the rebellion led by the Earl of Desmond, large tracts of Waterford, Cork, Kerry and Limerick were declared forfeit to the Crown. The territory was to be distributed among English planters, and detailed maps were essential for an orderly distribution. A commission was established to organise the surveying of the territory, and a number of professional surveyors were hired to oversee and carry out the work. Jobson was one of the most productive of the surveyors, but only a fraction of his output has survived. In addition to his plantation maps, he produced county maps of Limerick and Cork and this general map of Munster.

Jobson's large-scale maps drew heavily on his surveys and the areas which had been surveyed are represented in greater detail. The names of the Gaelicised lordships are given in bold lettering; the names of the main divisions of the province are displayed in decorative frames. They read, from left: Counte Desmound; Counte Kerre; Great Counte Lymerick; Smal Counte Lymrick; [?] Corke; Counte Teporare; Countie Waterfourd. Co. Clare is not included in the map as it was then considered part of Connacht.

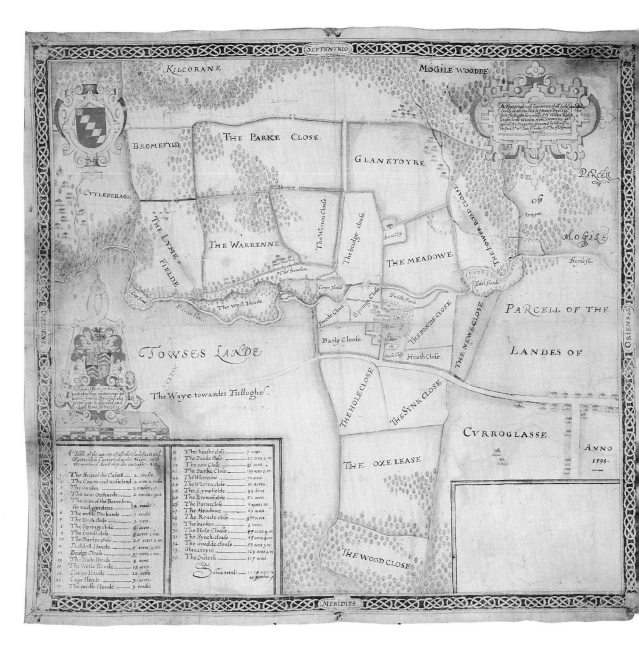

80 A manuscript estate map of Mogeely, Co. Cork, entitled, 'A topographical lineament of all such enclosed lands as are holden by Henrye Pyne, Esquire, from the Right Honourable Sir Walter Raley, Knight . . . as parcell of a seignorie graunted by Her Majestie to the said Sir Walter, late the lands of Sir John of Desmond, attainted', 1598. (54 x 48 cm; Ms 22,028.)

This is the earliest known Irish estate map. It was acquired with the Lismore Papers donated by the Duke of Devonshire in 1952. It depicts part of the lands forfeited by Sir John (FitzGerald) of Desmond, brother of the Earl of Desmond, mentioned in no. 79. The Earl, Sir John and other leaders of the rebellion lost their lands to English planters, of whom Sir Walter Raleigh is best known. Altogether, Sir Walter secured 40,000 acres in Waterford, Tipperary and Cork, including this estate of 1135 acres at Mogeely in East Cork which he leased to Henry Pyne.

The map is watercolour on vellum. It may have been drawn by John White of Virginia, an associate of Sir Walter Raleigh who is known to have lived for a time in Co. Cork. In style it is unique and does not fit into the Irish cartographic tradition.

81 Bird's-eye views by Richard Bartlett: Armagh City and a fort on the Blackwater, after July 1601. (40 x 27 cm; Ms 2656.)

Richard Bartlett was an English cartographer who accompanied Lord Deputy Mountjoy in the campaign against Hugh O'Neill in the period 1600-1603. He documented the campaign in a series of manuscript maps donated to the Library by Dr John Bowlby in 1955. It is probable that he was beheaded by the locals, seemingly because 'they would not have their country discovered'. Most of the maps are unfinished and the two cartouches in this specimen have not been filled in. Presumably such lavish productions were intended for presentation to some English dignitary of the period.

This fort on the Blackwater was begun in July 1601. It was not as well finished as the map suggests; it was an earth-work made by excavating ditches and throwing up the soil to form the parapets. The thatched houses within the fort are of a type then common in England; the circular thatched houses in Armagh are Irish. The building with the blue roof is the cathedral. Many of the other buildings are in ruins as Armagh was badly damaged a number of times in the wars of the previous fifty years; indeed, it was burnt by Hugh O'Neill in 1600 when it was under threat from Lord Mountjoy. The enclosures on the slopes of the hill with heaps of stones within them are probably the ruins of the 'trians', the thirds or districts of the ancient settlement of Armagh. The road at the top is the old road leading west; the circular structure at the top, just to the right of the road, is Emain Machae (Eamhain Macha – Navan Fort). The maps have been published in G.A. Hayes-McCoy, *Ulster and Other Irish Maps c. 1600*, Dublin, 1964.

186

Hugh O'Neill. (Hannibal Adami,
La Spada d'Orione Stellata, Rome, 1680.)

New fort of the Mullin

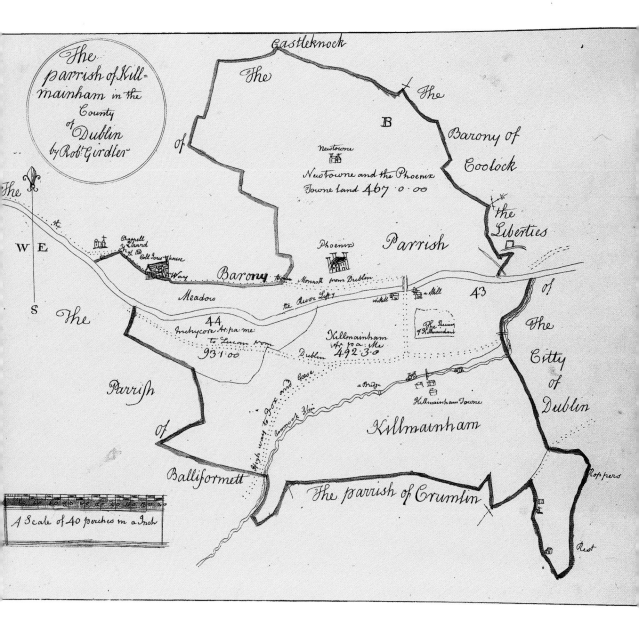

The parrish of Kill-
mainham in the
County
of Dublin
by Robᵗ Girdler

Castleknock

The

of

The

Barony of

Coolock

B

Newtowne

Newtowne and the Phoenix
Towne land 467 0 00

Parrish

the
Liberties

The

W E

S

N

Chappell
Izard

Ball Gore house

Way

Barony

Meadow

Phoenix

from Monnoth from Dublin

the River Liffi

a Mill

whell

43

of

The

Citty

of

Dublin

The

44

Inchycore A: pa me
to Lucan from
931 00

Dublin

Killmainham
A: to a: Me
4923 0

The Ruins
of Killmainham

Parrish

of

Balliformett

High way to Fox and Goose

Connock Hill

a Bridge

Killmainham Towne

Killmainham

The parrish of Crumlin

Roppers

Rest

A Scale of 40 porches in a Inch

188

82 William Petty's Down Survey 1655-57: 'The parish of Kilmainham, Co. Dublin', by Robert Girdler. (55 x 43 cm; Ms 714.)

The Down Survey was carried out to provide maps of lands forfeited to the Cromwellians in the 1650s. The maps were for use in dividing the lands among Cromwell's soldiers and the adventurers who financed his campaign in Ireland. The survey was organised by Sir William Petty, a remarkable Englishman who was then physician-in-chief to the forces in Ireland; he took on the commission as a speculative venture. It consisted of barony maps for most of the country and parish maps of the confiscated areas. Robert Girdler was one of Petty's team of 1,000 men and his name appears on a number of the maps. Most of the original maps were lost in fires; in 1969 the Library purchased a set of reliable copies for fourteen counties in Munster and Leinster and for Co. Leitrim. They were made in the late eighteenth century by a surveyor named Daniel O'Brien.

This parish map shows Kilmainham, bisected by the Liffey. An accompanying descriptive sheet or 'terrier' includes the following:

'. . . It contains the townlands of Kilmainham, Inchicore, Dolphin's Barn, the Phoenix and Newtown . . . On Kilmainham there stands the ruins of a large castle, a street of good habitable houses, two double mills and a single mill in repair, and an arched stone bridge across the River Liffey . . . At the Phoenix a very stately house now in good repair' [Phoenix Lodge, on the site of the Artillery Fort].

Petty used the data compiled in the course of the Down Survey to produce an atlas, *Hiberniae Delineatio* (1685) which includes the relatively accurate map of Ireland reproduced here.

189

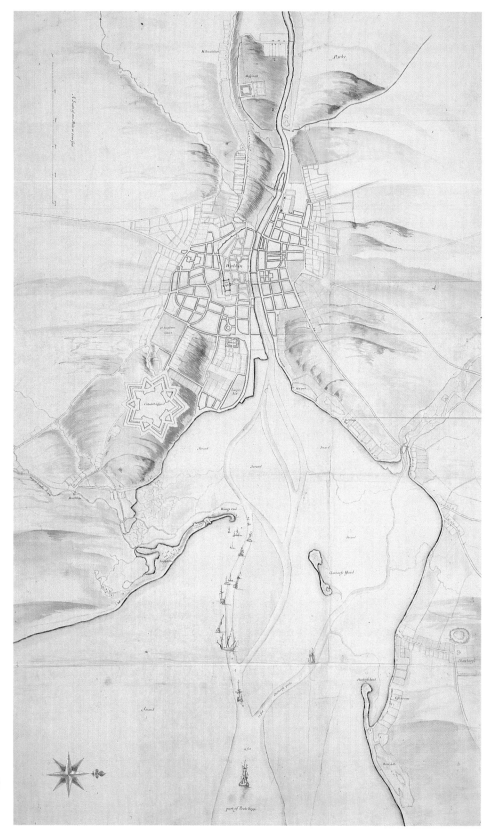

83 A manuscript map by Thomas Phillips, **'A Survey of the City of Dublin and Part of the Harbour below Ringsend',** 1685. (124 x 74 cm; Ms 2557.)

This map of Dublin is one of a series of manuscript maps and prospects of towns and fortifications by Thomas Phillips, a military engineer employed by James II in Ireland in 1685. The map is based on a survey made in 1673 by another official engineer, Sir Bernard de Gomme. The section reproduced includes the Royal Hospital at Kilmainham which opened in 1684. The great star-fort to the east of the city was never built.

   The maps and prospects are drawn in Indian ink with colour washes. The Library has two sets of Phillips' Irish maps and prospects, one acquired with the Ormond Papers in 1946 and the other purchased from the library of Sir Thomas Phillipps at Cheltenham (see also no. 37).

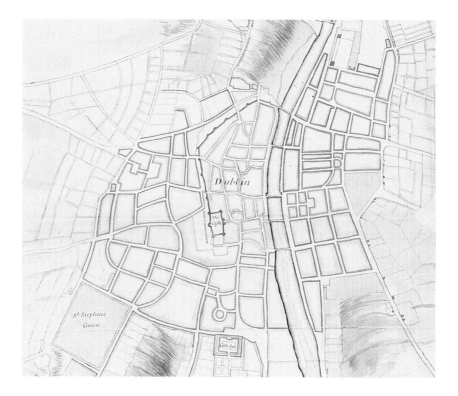

192

84 A volume of estate maps by John Rocque, **'A Survey of the Manor of Castledermot** situated in the County of Kildare belonging to the Right Honourable James, Earl of Kildare', 1758. (52 x 72 cm; Ms 22,003.)

This volume is one of a set of eight volumes of estate surveys produced by the French cartographer, John Rocque, for the Earl of Kildare in the period 1755-60. They were purchased by the Library in 1975. The volumes inaugurated the so-called 'French' style of land surveying in Ireland which featured elegant cartouches, marginal illustration and the use of colour to indicate land usage. Rocque is said to have charged the Earl only a hundred pounds for the surveys as he regarded estate surveying as a side-line to his main business which was concerned with printed maps of cities and towns.

This volume has ten coloured maps, including that of the town of Castledermot which is reproduced here. The table of reference gives the names of tenants and the valuation of tenements. It also includes other data, for instance, it lists three brew houses and four malt houses.

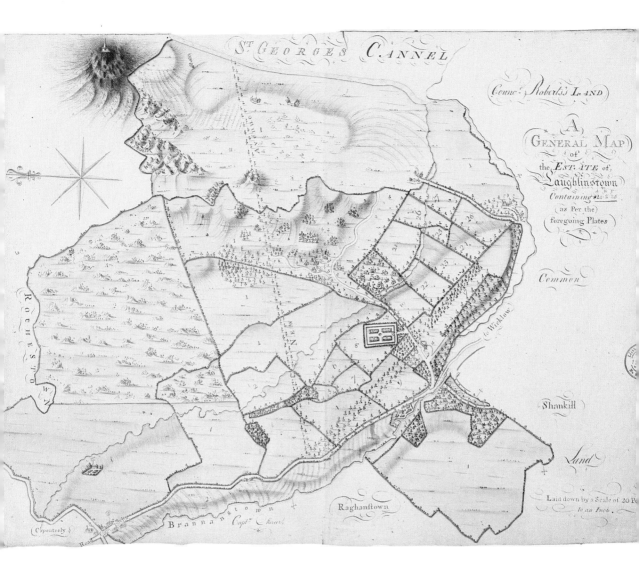

ST GEORGES CANNEL

Counc.r Roberts's Land

A
GENERAL MAP
of
the ESTATE of
Laughlinstown
Containing 124
as Per the
foregoing Plates

Common

to Wicklow

Shankill

Land

Laid down by a Scale of 20 Pe
to an Inch

ROCHESTOWN

Brannanstown Cap.tn Mercers

Raghanstown

Copventeely

Road

194

85 A volume of estate maps by Michael Kenny, **'A Book of Maps of the estate of the Reverend Doctor Domville** in the Counties of Meath, Dublin and Wexford', 1773. (53 x 73 cm; 21.F.108.)

The volume has thirty-eight coloured maps, including five by other surveyors. Nine of the maps relate to the estate at Loughlinstown in South County Dublin (off the Dublin to Bray road between Cabinteely and Shankill). The map reproduced here is a general map of the Loughlinstown estate which amounted to over eight hundred acres. The proprietor was the Rev. Benjamin Domvile, Rector of Bray and Prebendary of Rathmichael. He was born Barrington but took the name Domvile on inheriting the property (see also no. 21). The volume was acquired with the Domvile Papers which were acquired in the 1950s.

On the map relief is shown by a rather basic system of hachure (hill-shading). The different types of land are indicated by means of symbols and also by written descriptions on a reference page; for instance, the area below the compass star is 'scrubby, rocky pasture', while the area beneath it with the river flowing through is 'choice meadow'. The demesne is on the right hand side of the map, around the rectangular formal gardens. It includes orchards and gardens, groves of oak and ash, and a 'barcelona' plantation of hazel-nut trees imported from Spain. The 'New Avenue' running from top to bottom was never built. Loughlinstown House, to the right of the gardens, is now occupied by the European Foundation.

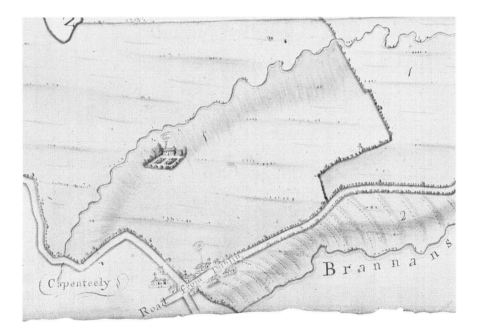

86 'Map of Ireland Exhibiting the Various Works in Operation', December 1847, published by the Board of Works, Ireland. (P.P. 1848, vol. xxxvii.)

This thematic map was published in the annual report of the Board of Works for 1847. It shows works sponsored by the Board and those for which it provided grants or loans. Schemes for drainage and land improvement accounted for £600,000 of the £1,000,000 represented. The emergency Famine relief schemes had closed down the previous summer as the government claimed they were no longer necessary; the Board was confined to the works shown here which were intended to provide permanent improvements.

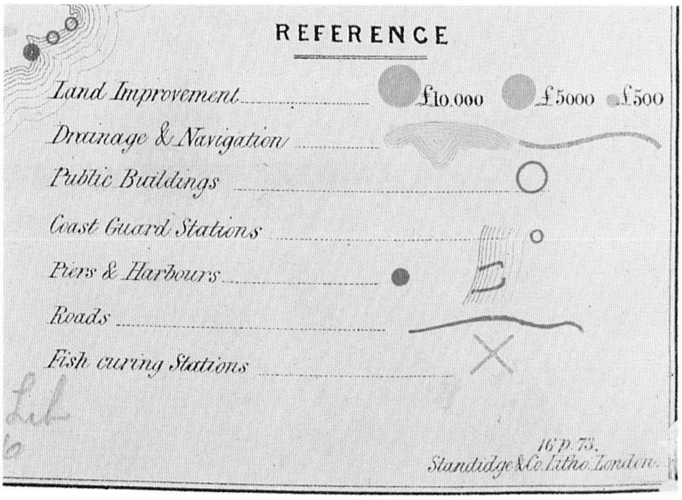

REFERENCE

Land Improvement £10,000   £5000   £500

Drainage & Navigation ....

Public Buildings ....

Coast Guard Stations ....

Piers & Harbours ....

Roads ....

Fish curing Stations ....

16 P. 73.
Standidge & Co. Litho London.

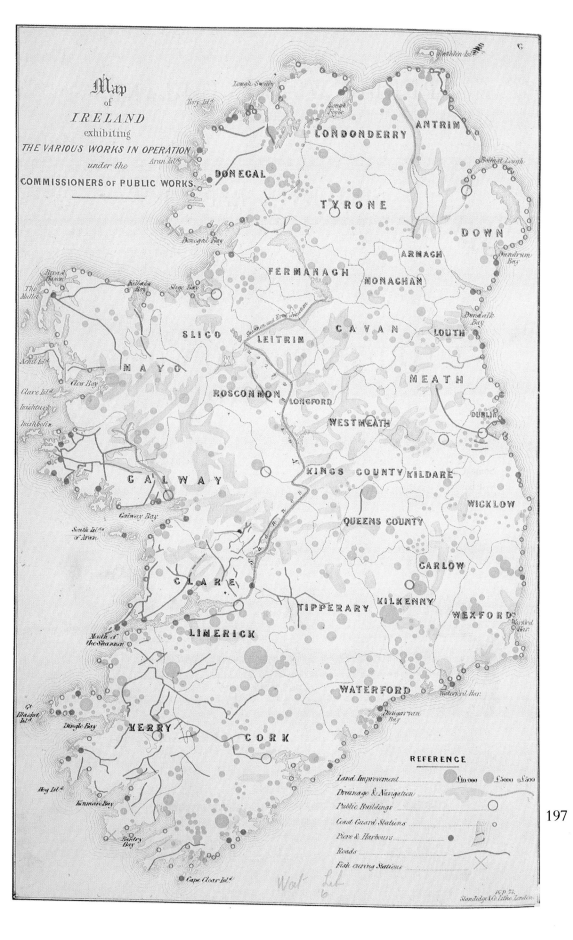

Map of IRELAND exhibiting THE VARIOUS WORKS IN OPERATION under the COMMISSIONERS of PUBLIC WORKS.

REFERENCE

Land Improvement £10,000 £5000 £500
Drainage & Navigation ....
Public Buildings ....
Coast Guard Stations ....
Piers & Harbours ....
Roads ....
Fish curing Stations ....

16 p 73.
Standidge & Co. litho London.

197

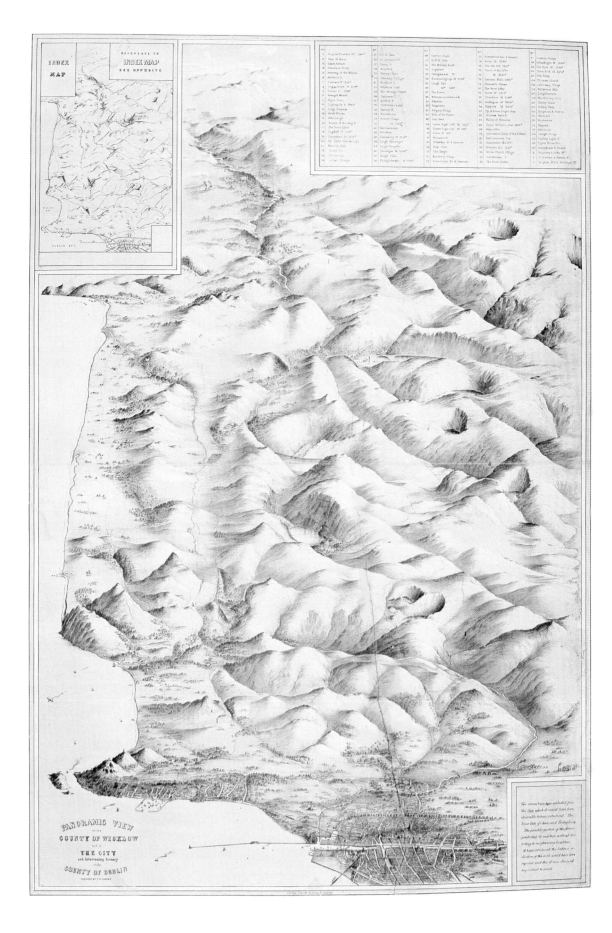

PANORAMIC VIEW
OF THE
COUNTY OF WICKLOW
and of
THE CITY
and Intervening Scenery
of the
COUNTY OF DUBLIN

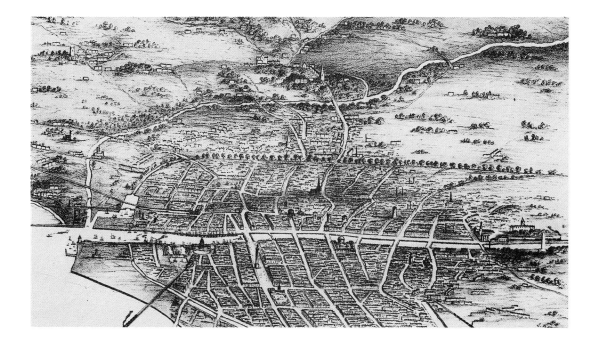

87 T. R. Harvey, **'Panoramic View of the County of Wicklow and of the City . . . of Dublin',** Dublin and London, *c.* 1850s. (1015 x 705 cm; 16.J.17.)

This panorama has some of the features of a map, but it is debateable whether it should be classified as a map as it is essentially an artist's impression. It is not, however, widely known and as a section of it now adorns the new Irish ten-pound note, people may find it of interest. The map was published in two editions, each with a booklet. The artist and author of the booklet, T. R. Harvey, writes that it was while he was at school at Nutgrove in Rathfarnham around 1843 that he conceived the idea of the panorama. The Library has two copies of the map and a copy of the booklet.

The structure of Dublin is clearly delineated; it is easy to find one's bearings from the three east-west lines representing the Liffey, the elms on the Grand Canal, and the River Dodder. Nelson's Pillar dominates the main artery of Sackville (O'Connell) Street – Grafton Street – Harcourt Street. To the west, the broad sweep of Capel Street – Parliament Street terminates at City Hall.

The roads leading to the country are easily identified. West of St Patrick's Cathedral, Patrick Street – New Street leads out to Rathfarnham. One can discern Rathmines Road and Rathgar Road; also Leeson Street leading from St Stephen's Green out to the bridge across the Dodder at Donnybrook. Kingstown (Dún Laoghaire) with its enclosed harbour appears as a considerable town. In the interests of clarity, certain features have been distorted; for instance, the height of the hills is exaggerated and the houses in the towns have been enlarged but reduced in number. Bray appears as a village when in fact it was then a town with over five hundred houses.

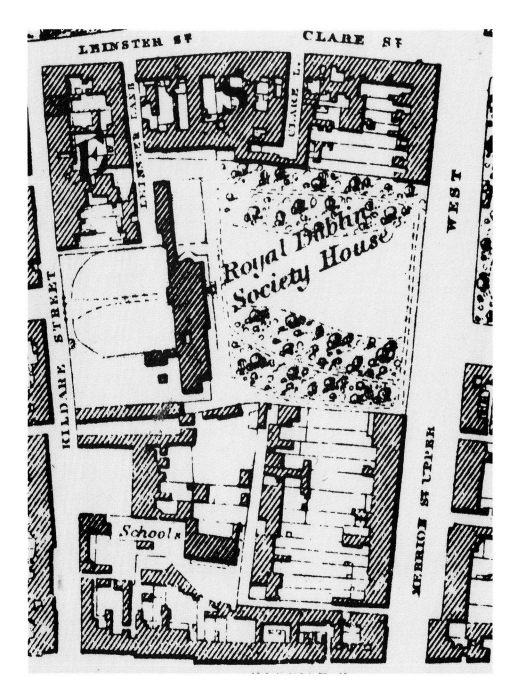

88 Sections of Ordnance Survey maps showing Kildare Street, the National Library and Leinster House in 1837 and 1935-36. (6-inch, enlarged, Dublin sheet 18.)

In the 1837 map, Leinster House is named as 'Royal Dublin Society House'. In the 1935-36 map, Leinster House is shown with a cultural institution erected in the interim period at each of its four corners – the National Library and the National

200

Museum on Kildare Street, and the National Gallery and the Natural History
Museum on Merrion Square; in addition, the Metropolitan School of Art (now the
National College of Art and Design) is located between the National Library and the
National Gallery. The Royal Dublin Society was instrumental in the foundation or
development of all these institutions in the period when it occupied Leinster House,
the grounds of which provided their sites.

201

X. THE GENEALOGICAL OFFICE*

by Donal F. Begley, Chief Herald of Ireland

In 1920 when Michael Collins directed one of his associates to keep a close eye on the Office of Arms, presumably his interest was not motivated by any desire to register a family tree or acquire a coat of arms. The future commander-in-chief of the army of the Irish Free State was, no doubt, aware of the close association of the Office of Arms, now the Genealogical Office, with the Lord Lieutenant's Household, both of which were located in Dublin Castle. The object of the exercise must have been to read the mind of the Establishment by closely monitoring the activities of the officers of arms at that critical moment in Irish history. Be that as it may, the episode is useful in demonstrating that the obligations and duties of the Ulster King of Arms arising out of his membership of the Vice-Regal Court, were, at least, on a par with his heraldic duties as set out in the patent of his creation. These twin historic functions of the Irish principal heralds determined in large measure the origin, nature and scope of such records as were made and maintained in the Irish Office of Arms.

Heraldry, as the reader will undoubtedly be aware, was a scientific system of symbolism under official control which had for its objective the identification of combatants in the peculiar conditions of medieval warfare. Characteristically, it was a system that was Christian, European, graphic, symbolic, territorial, and personal. It was controlled and regulated by a corps of professionals known as heralds who were usually appointed by royal decree.

In medieval times, principal heralds in England and on the Continent were given a territorial style or designation by their royal patrons. Heralds who had associations with Ireland were styled Ireland King of Arms, a title which after 1552 gave way to that of Ulster King of Arms. The explanation of the latter style may lie in the fact that the province of Ulster, originally granted to John de Courcey, had through a succession of heiresses long since resided in the Crown. The formal beginning of a heraldic authority for Ireland is grounded on what amounts to royal *fiat:* on 2 February 1552 King Edward VI wrote in his journal:

> 'There was a King of Arms made for Ireland whose name was Ulster, and his province was all Ireland, and he was the fourth King of Arms and the first herald of Ireland.'

In the same year, Bartholomew Butler was created King of Arms of all Ireland by letters patent, dated 1 June, and was granted:

> 'All rights, profits, commodities and emoluments in that office . . . with power . . . of inspecting, overseeing, correcting, and embodying the arms

*Reproduced from *Some Manuscript Treasures of the Genealogical Office* by Donal F. Begley, Dublin, 1994.

The Bedford Tower in Dublin Castle which accommodated the Office of Arms when it was reconstituted as the Genealogical Office in 1943; the Genealogical Office was relocated in 2-3 Kildare Street in 1987.

and ensigns of illustrious persons and of imposing and ordaining differences therein, according to the laws of arms; of granting letters patent of arms to men of rank and fit persons; and of doing . . . all things which by right or custom were known to be incumbent on the office of a king of arms'. In addition to his heraldic and genealogical duties the Ulster King of Arms also performed a number of exclusive official duties which resulted in his office becoming associated with the administration. A document entitled 'Duties and Services Performed by Ulster King of Arms', described him in the following terms:

'The first and only permanent officer of the Lord Lieutenant's Household in Ireland, with full responsibility for arranging all the public ceremonies connected with Government such as the proclamation of a new Sovereign, or peace, or war; the reception and inauguration of the Lord Lieutenant; custody of all records respecting such matters and keeping a record of all state proceedings'.

Thus, the functions of the principal herald of Ireland were twofold: first, to act as chief ceremonial functionary at the Vice-Regal Court, and second, to be the official overseer of heraldic matters in the new kingdom.

To the acquisitive Tudor kings, intent on bringing English influence to bear on their Irish possessions, the inception of a heraldic office for Ireland must have seemed a desirable, even a necessary, step. The opening in Dublin in 1541 of the Irish Parliament, modelled on the Westminster institution, required at local level a degree of expertise in protocol, procedure and ceremonial, supplied to the parliament in London by the College of Arms, which was not available in Ireland, and certainly not at an institutional level. The upgrading by Henry VIII of the constitutional status of Ireland from a lordship to a kingdom was marked symbolically by the official discarding of the symbol of the three crowns and by the reintroduction of the harp as the arms of Ireland. The regulation of such matters obviously required the presence of heralds, who were by tradition the established masters in the art and science of heraldry.

In the reign of Philip and Mary, a conscious policy of settling English people on the land of Ireland began to take shape with the plantation of part of the Midlands, thereafter known as King's and Queen's counties. In the circumstances of the time, some means had to be found to secure social acceptance for the Tudor 'new men'. Accordingly, heraldic patents were issued to the *novi homines* by the newly constituted Office of Arms. Exemplifications of arms found in the early registers of the Office reveal elaborate heraldic achievements with individual shields containing as many as a dozen charges. Many of these heraldic achievements reflect a preoccupation on the part of the grantees with family relationships expressed through the medium of impaling, quartering and cadency, not overlooking the heraldic pedigree. Because of the close association between the Office and the central government administration, entry in the heraldic register was a guarantee of high profile recognition. On the other hand, the heraldic register provided the authorities with a virtual 'Who's Who' of the wealthy and powerful in the new kingdom.

Given the nature of the relationship between the Office and the administration, it is only natural to expect that certain contemporary records should mirror the thinking of its political masters. It could not be otherwise. Certainly, this was true for sensitive periods, such as during the Reformation, the Nine Years War and the aftermath of the Battle of Kinsale. In one volume we find the arms of Hugh O'Neill defaced and underwritten with the word 'traytor'.

With the advent of the Stuart kings genuine initiatives in the area of heraldry

The State Heraldic Museum at 2-3 Kildare Street.

and genealogy resulted in the compilation of the Books of Heraldic Visitation and the Funeral Entry series – the latter being in the nature of a register of births, marriages and deaths, encompassing Gael, Norman and English, but, of course, confined to the nobility and gentry. The Office appeared to be taking a more detached stance and even during the unsettled Cromwellian period it continued to function normally, grants of arms being made by the Principal Herald of Ireland under the Commonwealth – the style of King of Arms was quietly dropped under the *res publica* regime. The fag-end of the Jacobite regime was to prove traumatic for the Office due to the divided loyalties of its staff, to the extent that a junior officer of arms of the day, James Terry, removed certain official books and the seal of the Office to the court of James II at Saint-Germain, where he continued to issue grants of arms in the name of the Stuart kings until his death in 1725.

The eighteenth century was an auspicious time for the Office, and the records of that period bespeak an augmentation, as it were, in the activities and responsibilities of the Officers of Arms. We now treat briefly of the events which led to the expansion in official activities. Following the Treaty of Limerick in 1691, the flower of the old nation in exile on the Continent found themselves part of a rigid aristocratic system where marriage into the local nobility, commissions in the army and admission to Court all depended on the possession of an attested family tree and an authentic coat of arms. Pedigrees were required to be authenticated by the competent authority in the home country and, in the course of a letter (29 March 1792) to Monsieur Henri Shee at the Palais Royal, Sir Chichester Fortescue wrote:

'If any family in France may in the future want the assistance of the Office of Arms to prove their kindred here, it would be well to correspond with the King of Arms . . . I as King of Arms have great pleasure in answering your letter . . .'

Of the pedigrees registered in the Office between 1750 and 1800, approximately fifty per cent appertain to the emigré families. It is a remarkable fact, and indeed a measure of its independence, that the Office was prepared to conduct so much business with the descendants of the Jacobite emigrés, who in the previous century had been dispossessed of their lands and sent into exile by the very political regime with which the Office itself, as we have seen, was so closely identified.

Under an act of parliament of 1707, the Office was given power to regulate membership of the Irish House of Lords. The act stipulated that, on the death of an Irish peer, his heirs were immediately to 'make an entry in the King of Arms Office' of the death, and also to provide other pertinent family information. The registration of this information gave rise to the keeping of a series of volumes entitled Lords Entries which contain detailed pedigrees and hand-painted arms of the Irish peers. The institution of an order of chivalry for Ireland in 1783, in the form of the Most Illustrious Order of St Patrick, had the effect of raising the public profile of the Office, a position which endured until 1921. Administration of the affairs of the Order was assigned by the Government to the Office of Arms which, perforce, became the registry of the Order. A long schedule of 'Patrick' duties included preparation for ceremonies of investiture and inauguration, the design and crafting of heraldic banners, and custody of the Grand Master's insignia which, as all the world knows, disappeared from the Office safe in 1907 during the tenure of Sir Arthur Vicars. The centrality of the Office in matters relating to the administration of the Order is attested by the records which include the Books of Investiture and Inauguration, four registers of knights and a volume of certificates of noblesse.

President John F. Kennedy receiving his patent of arms during his visit to Ireland in June 1963. The patent was prepared and signed by Mr Gerard Slevin, Chief Herald of Ireland.

Affairs of the Office during the nineteenth century and the records made during this period were dominated by the twin personalities of Sir William Betham and Sir Bernard Burke, one the great maker of records, the other the great arranger of archives. Betham was the first to take steps to popularise the Office and its services by placing public notices in the newspapers and we quote briefly from one such notice:

'The Herald's Office is now open to all and any man of any rank, whether entitled to bear arms or not, has a right to enrol his family in the records of the Office . . .'

Extant correspondence relating to the opening decades of the twentieth century foreshadows the demise of the old political order, and in 1921 all offices and services of the English administration in Ireland were transferred to the successor Irish government – with the exception of the Office of Arms. Over the following twenty years the constitutional position of the Office was the subject of intermittent discussion between the two governments until, finally, in 1943, following a mutually acceptable agreement, the Office and its contents were handed over to the Irish authorities. It was renamed the Genealogical Office, and its historic prerogatives in the matter of design, assignment and registration of heraldic property were confirmed by ministerial order.

The consolidation of the Office in the 1950s and 1960s was set against the background of what may be termed the 'roots' phenomenon, coupled with increasingly available world mobility. It fell to the Office to absorb the interest of an ever increasing segment of an Irish diaspora intent on taking a closer look at its Irish origins. With hindsight, the visit of President Kennedy to Ireland in 1963 may be seen as the *terminus a quo* of the modern 'roots' industry. The special disciplines of the Office were adapted with a view to making a significant contribution to the emerging national tourist effort. The importance of Irish genealogy in the context of tourism was brought sharply into focus in 1988 with the publication of a Bord Fáilte post-visitor survey which showed that thirty-six per cent of the visitors from North America who were interviewed indicated that tracing their Irish ancestry was either their primary or secondary reason for choosing Ireland as a holiday destination.

Today, in an age of internationalism and cultural common form, more people seem to want reassurance regarding those elements in their heritage which constitute their essential Irishness, that is to say, their family names, their lineage, their sense of place and the Irish language. The proven capacity of the Office to provide such reassurance to the Irish world at large is perhaps its forte.

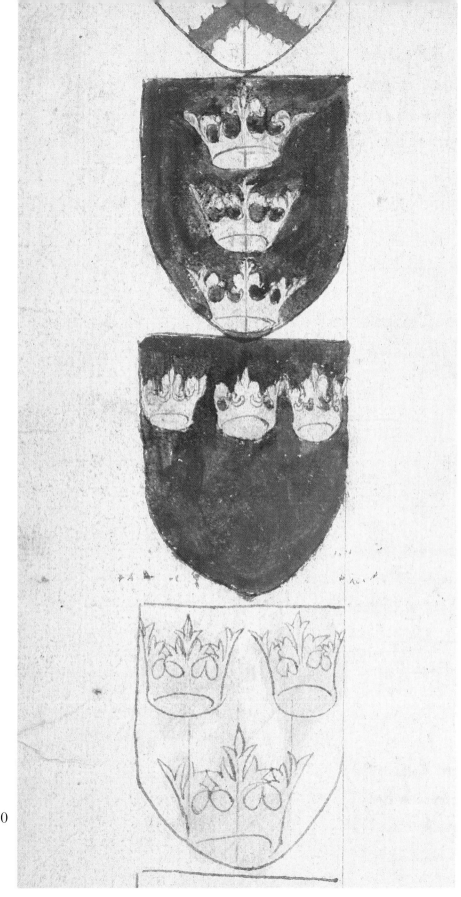

89 'A Treatise on Heraldry', 1345. (GO Ms 7.)

The manuscript is a compilation in Latin and English of portions of several medieval treatises on heraldry. It features blazons (verbal descriptions of arms) which are enhanced by coloured illustrations of the coats of arms of a number of medieval kingdoms and lordships. They include the lordship of Ireland which arose from a feudal grant of the country by Pope Adrian IV to King Henry II of England in the twelfth century.

The symbol of the crowns in triplicate served as the mark of the lordship of Ireland in late-medieval times and was probably inspired by the papal tiara. In the manuscript the artist seems to be considering possible arrangements of the crowns. The triple-crown device featured prominently on the coinage of Ireland until the time of Henry VIII; it was later used in modified form (antique crowns) as the arms of the province of Munster, here illustrated in a modern map representing the ancient divisions of Ireland.

211

Hibernia insula in Ociano Septentrionabi tantum fere aBritania, distans, quantum Britania a continente Inuen: Sati 2 plumis Hiberniã vocat: Claudianus in quarto honorü consulatat Iernam hodie vulgi vocabulo Irlandia nominatur.

90 'Irish Nobility', 1597–1603. (GO Ms 34.)

This manuscript contains emblazoned achievements of members of the nobility of Ireland during the reign of Queen Elizabeth I. It also includes the depiction of the dynastic symbols of Ireland, ancient, medieval and modern, reproduced here. The devices on the banner on the right (an ancient house, a stag issuant therefrom, and four trees) allude to the early Gaelic myth where a candidate for kingship pursues an enchanted deer into the house of the future king. A more conventional rendering of this motif now constitutes the crest of Ireland, here seen on a wreath atop a helmet. The 'majesty' featured on the banner on the left was widely acknowledged in texts of the later Middle Ages as a heraldic expression of the kingship of Ireland.

The earliest reference to the harp as the arms of Ireland is found in a thirteenth-century French roll of arms now preserved in The Hague in Holland. The entry reads, *Le Roi d'Irlande: D'azur à la harpe d'or;* this is precisely the blazon or technical description of the presidential flag as used today. The harp was used as the arms of Ireland from the time of Henry VIII; a wooden plaque bearing the device was displayed over the Speaker's chair in the Irish House of Commons in the period before the Act of Union. The plaque (reproduced here) is now in the State Heraldic Museum.

91 The initial volume of the **'Funeral Entry Books of Ireland'** series, 1588-1617. (GO Ms 64.)

The volumes of funeral entries were made following decrees of state which required that, on the death of prominent individuals, details regarding their families, arms and heirs be filed with the Office of Arms. The series is a prime source for the study of family history in the seventeenth century.

   The plan reproduced here is part of the funeral entry of Elizabeth, Countess of Ormond, wife of Thomas Butler ('Black Tom'), Tenth Earl of Ormond. It shows the altar table, canopy and enclosure in 'the Cathedrall Church of Kilkenny, the 21 of Aprill anno 1601', where the Countess was buried. An ubiquitous feature of the display is the coat of arms, ensigned with an earl's coronet, of Butler, Earls of Ormond (whence the modern sporting colours of Co. Tipperary), impaled with the three sheaves of Baron Sheffield, father of the Countess. The banners at the corners of the enclosure carry the impaled arms of a number of her exclusively English ancestors.

A seventeenth-century representation of the principal Butler castle. (Thomas Dingley, *Tour in Ireland, c.* 1681.)

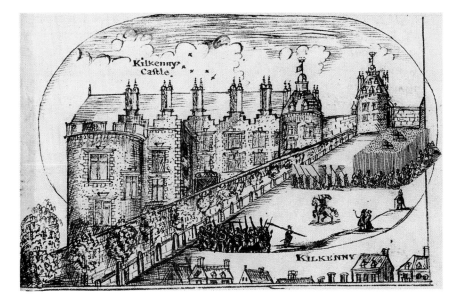

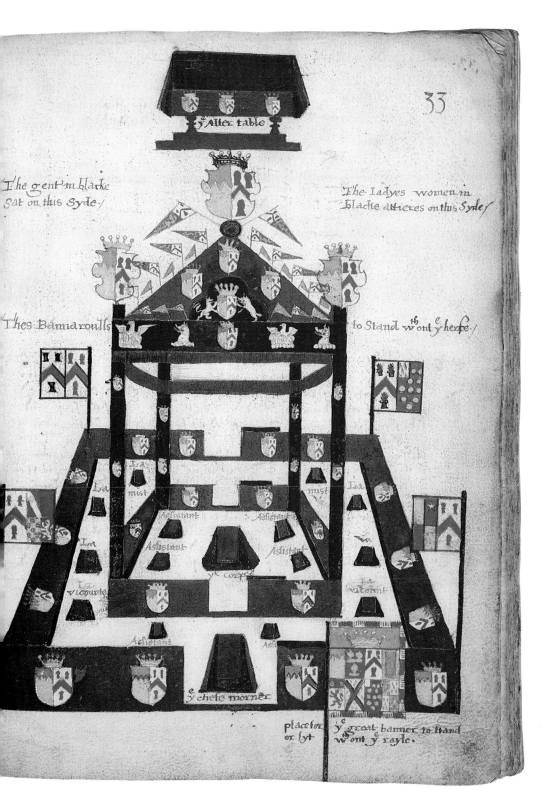

ye Alter table

The gent' in blacke Sat on this Syde.

The ladyes women in blacke attieres on this Syde

Thes Bannaroulls

to Stand wthont ye hexse

La. mist

La.

Assistant

Assistant

Assistant

Assistant

mist

La.

La.

ye corpse

La. vicounte

La. vicount

Assistant

Ass

ye chefe morner

place for or syt

ye great banner to stand wthont ye rayle.

A

VISITATION BEGONNE
IN THE CITTIE OF
DVBLIN BY DANIELL
MOLYNEVX ESQVIRE,
OTHERWISE CALLED
VLSTER KINGE OF
ARMES AND PRINCI-
PALL HERALD OF ALL
IRELAND, IN THE
YEERE OF GRACE
ONE THOVSAND
SIX HVNDRETH
AND SEVEN, AS
FOLOWETH

216

92 'The Books of Heraldic Visitation': the volume for 1607. (GO Ms 46.)

The heralds' visitations were undertaken, 'to observe the arms . . . of all noblemen . . . and to correct all false armour and all such as without their consent do presume to bear arms . . .' In February 1607, the Ulster King of Arms, Daniel Molyneux, undertook a visitation of the country at large, beginning with the city of Dublin. This manuscript is the official record of arms authenticated by him in the course of that visitation.

The volume includes the exemplification of the arms of the city of Dublin here reproduced – three blazing castles on an azure background. The choice of a castle as a heraldic device for the civic arms was almost certainly inspired by the thirteenth-century seal matrix of the city which features a triple-towered fortified structure being defended under siege. The flammant castles probably reflect the turbulent beginnings of the city which withstood a number of assaults. The castles are triplicated according to heraldic convention which required balance and symmetry in design and layout. The heraldic supporters on either side of the shield are holding symbols of Law and Justice and laurel branches.

The motto obviously did not find favour with Bernard Burke, Ulster King of Arms (died 1892), because of its poor Latinity; he corrected it to read, *Obedientia Civium Urbis Felicitas* (the well-being of the city depends on the co-operation of its citizens).

Knightes Dubbed by the right honorable
Sᵣ Arthure Chichester knight, Lo: Dep: ⫻ ⫻
of Ireland. Sworn yᵉ third of Febuarⁱⁱ 1604ꝯ

Care Cheerish truth ⫽
Honor Sequitur Fugientem

Sir Arthur Chichester from a contemporary engraving; he acquired extensive estates in counties Antrim, Derry and Donegal.

93 'Knights Dubbed in Ireland', 1565-1616. (GO Ms 49.)

This manuscript is a contemporary register which lists the names, dates, places of creation, and coats of arms of knights dubbed in Ireland in the period 1565-1615. In addition, it records the names and arms of the several Lords Deputy who conferred the honours on behalf of the English monarchs. In the case of a number of Gaelic lords who were reluctantly knighted no entries occur for their arms. The perceived effect of knighthood was to raise the individual's social status to a degree above the rank of gentleman.

The heraldic achievement reproduced here is that of Sir Arthur Chichester, Lord Deputy in the period 1605-15. It shows the descent and alliances of his family through the medium of heraldic quarterings which represent the following families, beginning with the pronominal: Chichester, Raleigh, Stockley, Penrell, Gorges, Walkingham, [?], Willington, Wise. It is a good example of what may be termed court heraldry as opposed to the simple military shields of the medieval period of heraldry.

94 **'Monumenta Eblanae'** [Dublin monuments], *c.* 1590-1650. (GO Ms 14.)

Heralds were generally entitled to certain emoluments for attendance at obsequies, and on such occasions probably arranged for a sketch of the funeral monument to be made for the Office of Arms. The manuscript, 'Monumenta Eblanae', is a collection of sketches of funeral monuments featuring armorial achievements in a number of Dublin churches. The page selected shows the monument in St Patrick's Cathedral to Thomas Jones (1550?-1619), Archbishop of Dublin and Lord Chancellor of Ireland.

At the top is a delineation of the shield, crest and supporters of Jones, Viscounts Ranelagh. In the panel immediately below, Archbishop Jones is portrayed facing the Lord Chancellor's purse with the royal arms theron. The reclining figure in armour in the large panel represents his son, Roger Jones, Viscount Ranelagh, who died in 1644. Also depicted are Roger's two wives at prayer, with their coats of arms on oval cartouches above; other members of the family are to the left and right.

St Patrick's Cathedral. (Thomas Dingley, *Tour in Ireland, c. 1681.)*

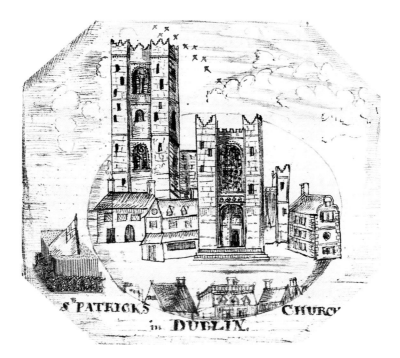

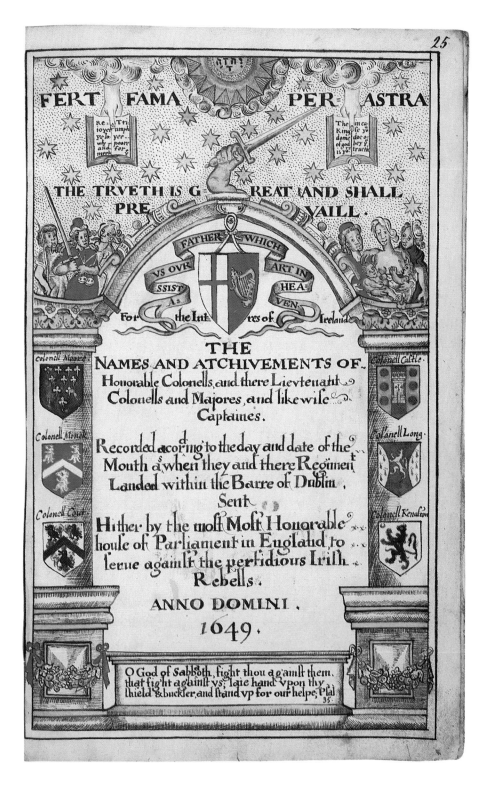

FERT FAMA PER ASTRA

THE TRVETH IS GREAT AND SHALL PREVAILL.

OVR FATHER WHICH ART IN HEAVEN ASSIST:

For the Inte...res of Ireland

Colonell Moore

Colonell Monck

Colonell Coot

Colonell Castle

Colonell Long

Colonell Kendrick

THE
NAMES AND ATCHIVEMENTS OF

Honorable Colonells, and there Lievtenant Colonells and Majores, and likewise Captaines.

Recorded acoring to the day and date of the Mouth a when they and there Regiment Landed within the Barre of Dublin.

Sent

Hither by the most Most Honorable house of Parliament in England to serue against the perfidious Irish Rebells.

ANNO DOMINI.

1649.

O God of Sabboth, fight thou against them, that fight against vs, laie hand vpon thy shield & buckler, and stand vp for our helpe, Psal 35.

95 'British Families', Vol. III, *c.* 1655. (GO Ms 44.)

The series records the heraldic bearings of a number of the higher officers of Cromwell's army in Ireland. It was made in the tenure of office of Richard Carney who was appointed Principal Herald by Cromwell in 1655.

The title page is a curious amalgam of Christian symbolism, classical heraldry and later medieval iconography. At the top is a representation of the *Kabod* or radiance of the Godhead, on either side of which is a hand descending from clouds holding an open book symbolising the Old and New Testaments. In the honour point of the page is the Union shield of the Commonwealth of England and Ireland, depicting the cross of St George of England impaled with the Irish harp. On the columns are the shields of arms of the well-known Cromwellian army officers, Moore, Monck, Coote, Castle, Long and Kenalton.

This detail from the manuscript is based on the legend of St George and the Dragon.

96 Confirmation of arms of Daniel O'Donnell (Domhnall Ó Domhnaill) of
Ramelton, Co. Donegal, by James Terry, Athlone Herald at the Jacobite Court of
Saint-Germain-en-Laye, 5 April 1709.

The confirmation includes a recitation of the genealogy of Daniel O'Donnell,
nobleman, son of Terence (Toirdhealbhach) of Ramelton, Co. Donegal, and kinsman
of Rory O'Donnell, Earl of Tyrconnell, who died in Rome on 28 July 1608. The
purpose of the document was to confirm the arms of the Earl (*sans* supporters and
coronet) to the aforesaid Daniel. The item shows obvious signs of bleaching, due no
doubt to prolonged exposure to sunlight at some period in its history. The detail here
reproduced is an exemplification of the full armorial achievement of the Earl, Rory
O'Donnell, dated 1607. It is interesting to note that the emblem of the bull is a
prominent feature on the seal of Red Hugh (Aodh Ruadh) O'Donnell, brother of
Rory, impressions of which are found on the correspondence of Red Hugh in the
archives of Simancas in Spain.

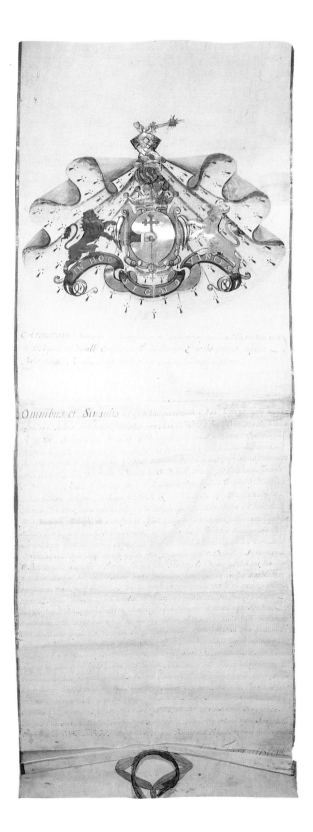

Genealogia ... et Insignia
Bernardi Maguire, ... Nobilis quem unicum
habuit filium et heredem ... Bryanus Maguire, armiger.

Genealogy and Ensigns armorial of Bernard Maguire, gentleman.

The Blazoning of the honble. family of Maguire, lords of Fermanagh, in the province of Ulster, in the Kingdom of Ireland.

Arms of O'Hayden, of the province of Munster, in the Kingdom of Ireland.

97 A nineteenth-century copy by William Williams of **Charles Lynegar's genealogy of Bernard Maguire,** 1731.

Charles Lynegar was of the family of Ó Luinín, by tradition family historians to the Maguires of Fermanagh. On taking the post of Professor of Irish at Trinity College, Dublin, in 1712, he considered it expedient to use an anglicised form of his name. In the preamble to the genealogy, which was almost certainly a commissioned work, he describes himself as Chief Antiquary of Ulster and all Ireland, thus mirroring the style and title of the head of the Office of Arms.

The genealogy is in Irish, Latin, English and French and purports to show the descent of Bernard Maguire, a member of a family latterly of Clonea, Co. Waterford, from a fifteenth-century ancestor, Tomás Mór MagUidhir, King of Fermanagh, whose descent in turn is set forth from Conn of the Hundred Battles. The detail reproduced shows the bearings of Maguire impaling those of Hayden, symbolising the marriage of Bryan Maguire to Catherine Hayden in the seventeenth century.

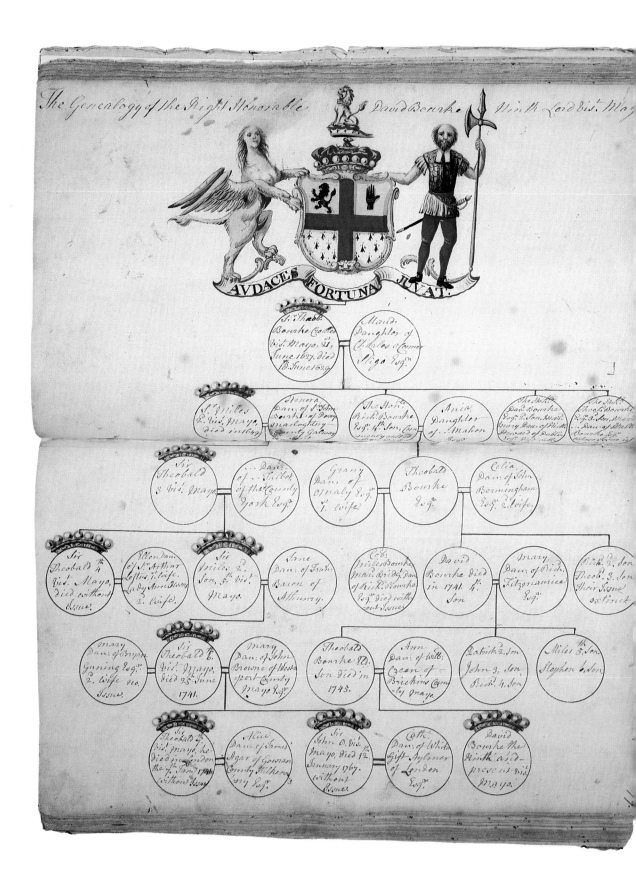

The Genealogy of the Right Honorable David Bourke Ninth Lord Vis. Mayo

AVDACES FORTUNA JUVAT.

98 'Registered Pedigrees', *c.* 1750–1800. (GO Ms 165.)

The Registered Pedigrees series is one of four official sets of registers which derive from the historic functions of the Office of Arms, the others being the Register of Arms, the Books of Heraldic Visitation and the Funeral Entry Books of Ireland. The manuscript is largely a register of patents and certificates issued by the Office of Arms during the second half of the eighteenth century to Irish noblemen on the Continent, particularly in Spain, France and Austria.

The pages reproduced feature an exemplification of the arms of Burke, Viscounts Mayo, followed by a genealogical chart showing descent from Theobald Burke ('Teabóid na Long'), First Viscount Mayo (created 1627), son of Sir Richard Burke and Grace O'Malley (Gráinne Mhaol), down to David, the Ninth Viscount who died in 1790. The heraldic achievement and genealogy is evidence of the acceptance by the Office of Arms of the claims of the Ninth Viscount Mayo to be recognised as such at a time when his status was being questioned by the peerage authorities in England.

The volume of pedigrees is mainly devoted to the descendants of 'Wild Geese', many of whom served in Irish regiments in the French army as illustrated in this contemporary French print.

REGIMENTS IRLANDAIS

Edward the Seventh, by the Grace of God of the United Kingdom of Great Britain and Ireland and of the British Dominions beyond the Seas, King, Defender of the Faith, Emperor of India, Sovereign and Chief of the Most Distinguished Order of Saint Michael and Saint George, to Our Trusty and Well-beloved Roger Casement, Esquire, lately Our Consul in the Congo Free State,

Greeting.

Whereas We have thought fit to nominate and appoint you to be a Member of the Third Class or Companions of Our Most Distinguished

Grant of the Dignity of a

Companion   of the Most Distinguished Order of Saint Michael and Saint George to Roger Casement, Esquire.

99 Roger Casement's award and insignia of the Most Distinguished Order of Saint Michael and Saint George, 30 June 1905. (State Heraldic Museum.)

In the course of his life Sir Roger Casement was awarded three official British honours – the Queen's South African Medal in 1903, membership of the Most Distinguished Order of Saint Michael and Saint George in 1905, and a knighthood in 1911. He renounced his honours in 1915 and was officially stripped of them on his conviction for treason in 1916.

Membership of the Order of Saint Michael and Saint George is usually reserved for those who have performed with distinction in the British foreign service. It was given to Casement for his work as Consul in the Congo Free State where his disclosures on maladministration attracted international attention. As an Irish nationalist, Casement had mixed feelings about the award; he chose not to accept it personally, and did not open the postal packet containing the insignia.

Casement's award was a C.M.G. (Companion of the Order), and is the lowest of three grades. The Order's emblem at the head of the document features St Michael and St George.

100 Copy of **Certificate of Recognition of Ó Dochartaigh (O'Doherty) of Inis Eoghain,** Co. Donegal, Chief of the Name, 1990.

The certificate of recognition was the official instrument which passed the Genealogical Office to Señor Ramón O Dogherty of Cádiz, Spain, formally accepting his petition to be recognised as the genealogically pre-eminent representative of his name. The document attests his descent in unbroken succession from Niall Noígiallach (Niall of the Nine Hostages), King of Tara (*floruit* fifth century A.D.). The pedigree was the culmination of in-depth research in a wide range of Gaelic and post-Gaelic manuscript sources undertaken by the Office.

The shield in the upper left embodies the ancient arms of Ó Dochartaigh; that on the right was conceded in 1790 by Sir Chichester Fortescue, Ulster King of Arms, to the sons of Eoghan Ó Dochartaigh, Henry, John and Clinton; they had been brought to Spain shortly before that date by their uncle Henry, then vicar-general of the diocese of Meath.

Ancient

Míl Espáine : Míl de Esp
ónan shíolnaigh de réin Leabhan C
de guien desciende según Leabhan

Niall Noígiallach
Rí Teamhnach : Rey de Ta
ófit ca. 450 A.D.

Conall Gulban
a quo
Cenél Conaill

Feagus Cendfota

Sétnae

Lugaid

Rónán

Garb

Cenn Fáelad

Fiaman
a quo
Clann Fiamhain

Máengal

Burt Castle, an Ó Dochartaigh fortress on the shores of Lough Swilly. (Based on an original in State Papers Ireland, April-May 1601, and reproduced from a re-drawing in *Ulster Journal of Archaeology,* 1939.)

Ó DOCHARTAIGH INIS EOGHAIN

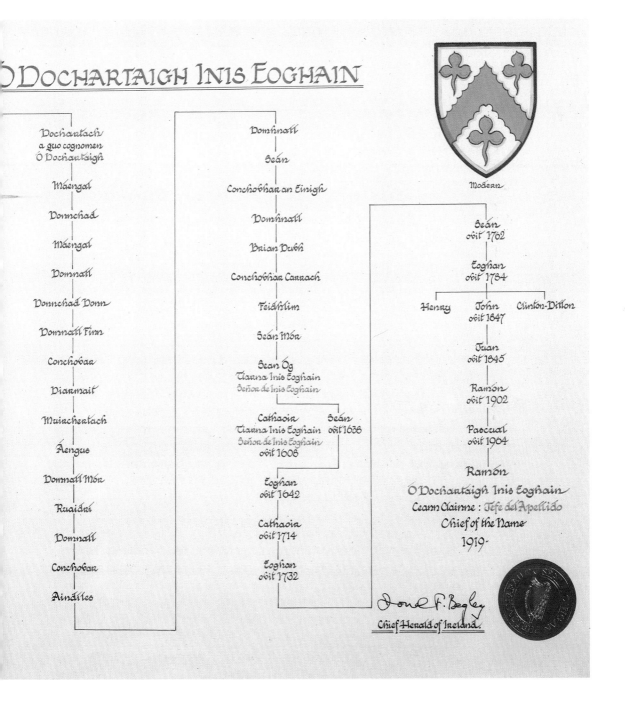

Dochartach
a guo cognomen
Ó Dochartaigh

Máengal

Donnchad

Máengal

Domnall

Donnchad Donn

Domnall Finn

Conchobar

Diarmait

Muirchertach

Áengus

Domnall Mór

Ruaidrí

Domnall

Conchobar

Aindíles

Domhnall

Seán

Conchobhar an Einigh

Domhnall

Brian Dubh

Conchobhar Carrach

Feidhlim

Seán Mór

Sean Óg
Tiarna Inis Eoghain
Señor de Inis Eoghain

Cathaoir   Seán
Tiarna Inis Eoghain   obit 1638
Señor de Inis Eoghain
obit 1608

Eoghan
obit 1642

Cathaoir
obit 1714

Eoghan
obit 1732

Modern

Seán
obit 1762

Eoghan
obit 1784

Henry   John   Clinton-Dillon
             obit 1847

Juan
obit 1845

Ramón
obit 1902

Pascual
obit 1964

Ramón
Ó Dochartaigh Inis Eoghain
Ceann Cláirne : Jefe del Apellido
Chief of the Name
1919-

Donl. F. Begley
Chief Herald of Ireland.

233

USING THE NATIONAL LIBRARY

The National Library is a cultural institution under the aegis of the Department of Arts, Culture and the Gaeltacht. Its mission is to collect and preserve books, manuscripts and illustrative material of Irish interest and make them accessible to the public. The one hundred treasures described in this book are all of exceptional interest, but each of the several million other items in the collections also has significance. In a library context, an item which is regarded as commonplace by most people may well be considered a treasure by somebody with some special interest. In this way, the treasures featured in this book are not usually the focus of attention for the hundreds of readers who visit the Library every day; instead, most of the readers are in search of some information which can be provided by one or other of the more mundane sources. Altogether, the readers seem to have a virtually infinite variety of interests, and they include those engaged in long-term research with an eye to a book or article and those with a once-off specific need – for instance, a person may want to check a newspaper report on a traffic accident for use in a court case.

The National Library is open, free of charge, to all who want to use it. There is a brief interview to establish the identity of the prospective reader and also to ensure that the items required are actually in the Library, and that they are not more readily accessible in the person's local public library. The applicant is then given a Reader's Ticket which has to be shown each day on entering the Library. For those who want to read manuscripts or other unique or rare items, a special Reader's Ticket is necessary; this may be got by applying to the staff responsible for the particular collection.

The Library does not lend books and reading is done in the various reading rooms. There is also a copying service and it is possible to get photocopies, photographs, slides or microfilms of most items in the collections. The Library has an on-going programme of exhibitions, for instance, the *Treasures* exhibition mounted in 1994. Facsimile versions of some of the exhibitions are toured and displayed at libraries, museums, heritage centres and other venues around the country. A book, booklet, catalogue or folder of facsimile documents is published in conjunction with certain exhibitions. Some of these are specifically designed for use in schools, but others are of general interest. A number of the titles are listed under *Suggested Reading* on page 236. The travelling exhibitions and the publications enable people at a distance from Dublin to derive some benefit from the National Library which is intended to serve all the people of Ireland and, indeed, anybody else who wishes to use it.

Readers will note that many of the treasures described in the book have been generously donated. Throughout its history, the National Library has been very fortunate in attracting donations of books, manuscripts and other items, and once again acknowledges the contribution made by thousands of donors in building up the collections. Donations of material are always most welcome; in addition, those wishing to make a financial contribution towards the work of the National Library by donation or bequest may do so through the National Library of Ireland Trust. There is also a support group, the National Library of Ireland Society, which is concerned with promoting and publicising the Library. Membership is open to readers or others with an interest in the National Library and the heritage in its care.

SUGGESTED READING

John H. Andrews, *Irish maps*, Dublin, Eason, Irish Heritage Series, 1978.
  Plantation acres. An historical study of the Irish land surveyor and his maps, Belfast, 1985.
Nicholas Barker, *Portrait of an obsession: The life of Sir Thomas Phillipps* (an adaptation from five volumes of Phillipps Studies by A. N. L. Munby), London, 1967.
Edward Chandler and Peter Walsh, *Through the brass-lidded eye*, Dublin, 1989.
Maurice Craig, *Irish bookbindings*, Dublin, Eason, Irish Heritage Series, 1976.
Catherine Fahy, *W. B. Yeats and his circle*, Dublin, 1989.
Peter Fox (ed.), *Treasures of the Library, Trinity College Dublin*, Dublin, 1986.
Bamber Gascoigne, *How to identify prints*, London, 1986.
Peter Harbison, *Beranger's views of Ireland*, Dublin, Royal Irish Academy, 1991.
Patrick Henchy, *The National Library of Ireland 1941-1976: A look back*, Dublin, National Library of Ireland Society, 1986.
Kieran Hickey, *The light of other days: Irish life at the turn of the century in the photographs of Robert French*, London, 1973.
John Killen, *A history of the Linen Hall Library 1788-1988*, Belfast, 1990.
Noel Kissane, *The National Library of Ireland*, Dublin, Eason, Irish Heritage Series, 1984.
  The Irish face, Dublin, 1986.
  Ex camera 1860-1960: Photographs from the collections of the National Library of Ireland, Dublin, 1990.
Paul Larmour, *The arts & crafts movement in Ireland*, Belfast, 1992.
Muriel McCarthy, *All graduates and gentlemen: Marsh's Library*, Dublin, 1980.
Dermot McGuinne, *Irish type design: A history of printing types in the Irish character*, Dublin, Irish Academic Press, 1992.
James Meenan and Desmond Clarke, *The Royal Dublin Society 1731-1981*, Dublin, 1981.
Nessa Ní Shéaghdha, *Collectors of Irish manuscripts: Motives and methods*, Dublin Institute for Advanced Studies, 1985.
Brian Ó Cuív, *The Irish bardic duanaire or poem-book*, (for the R. I. Best Memorial Trust), Dublin, [1973?].
John O'Meara, *Giraldus Cambrensis (Gerald of Wales): The history and topography of Ireland . . . translated from the Latin*, Mountrath, 1982.
Hugh Oram, *The advertising book: The history of advertising in Ireland*, Dublin, 1996.
  The newspaper book: A history of newspapers in Ireland 1649-1983, Dublin, 1983.
James O'Toole, *NEWSPLAN: Report of the Newsplan Project in Ireland*, Dublin and London, 1992.
Adrian Wilson, *The making of the Nuremberg Chronicle*, Amsterdam, 1976.
National Library *Folders of Facsimile Documents;* there are eleven titles in print, including the following: *The Landed Gentry* (1977).
                                                    Daniel O'Connell (1978).
                                                    Ireland from Maps (1980).
                                                    Athbheochan na Gaeilge (1981).
                                                    Grattan's Parliament (1982).
                                                    Historic Dublin Maps (1988).

INDEX